FOLK-TALES OF THE KHASIS

FOLK-TALES OF THE KHASIS

BY

MRS. RAFY

GYAN

Published by

GYAN

Gyan Publishing House
5, Ansari Road
Daryaganj, New Delhi-110002
Phone: 011-47034999, 9811692060
E-mail: books@gyanbooks.com

Distribution Network
gyanbooks.com
India, USA, Canada, UK, Australia, France

ISBN: 978-81-212-7200-1 (PB)
First Published, 1920

2nd Impression 2023

Printed at: Gyan Press, Delhi.

FOLK-TALES OF THE KHASIS
Author: MRS. RAFY

FOLK-TALES OF THE KHASIS

IN THE NEIGHBOURHOOD OF THE MOUNTAIN OF THE IEI TREE.

FOLK-TALES OF THE KHASIS

BY

MRS. RAFY

ILLUSTRATED

MACMILLAN AND CO., LIMITED
ST. MARTIN'S STREET, LONDON
1920

CONTENTS

ILLUSTRATIONS

I

WHAT MAKES THE ECLIPSE

VERY early in the history of the world a beautiful female child, whom the parents called Ka Nam, was born to a humble family who lived in a village on the borders of one of the great Khasi forests. She was such a beautiful child that her mother constantly expressed her fears lest some stranger passing that way might kidnap her or cast an "evil eye" upon her, so she desired to bring her up in as much seclusion as their poor circumstances would permit. To this the father would not agree; he told his wife not to harbour foolish notions, but to bring up the child naturally like other people's children, and teach her to work and to make herself useful. So Ka Nam was brought up like other children, and taught to work and to make herself useful.

One day, as she was taking her pitcher to the well, a big tiger came out of the forest and carried her to his lair. She was terrified almost to death, for she knew that the tigers were the most cruel of all beasts. The name of this tiger was U Khla, and his purpose in carrying off the maiden was to eat her, but when he saw how young and small she was, and that she would not suffice for one full meal for him, he decided to keep her in his lair until she grew bigger.

He took great care of her and brought home to her many delicacies which her parents had never been able to afford, and as she never suspected the cruel designs of the tiger, she soon grew to feel quite at home and contented in the wild beast's den, and she grew up to be a maiden of unparalleled loveliness.

The tiger was only waiting his opportunity, and when he saw that she had grown up he determined to kill her, for he was longing to eat the beautiful damsel whom he had fed with such care. One day, as he busied himself about his lair, he began to mutter to himself: "Now the time has come when I can repay myself for all my trouble in feeding this human child; to-morrow I will invite all my fellow-tigers here and we will feast upon the maiden."

It happened that a little mouse was foraging near the den at that time and she overheard the tiger muttering to himself. She was very sorry for the maiden, for she knew that she was alone and friendless and entirely at the mercy of the tiger; so the little mouse went and told the maiden that the tigers were going to kill her and eat her on the following day. Ka Nam was in great distress and wept very bitterly. She begged of the mouse to help her to escape, and the mouse, having a tender heart, gave her what aid was in her power.

In the first place she told the maiden to go out of the den and to seek the cave of the magician, U Hynroh, the Giant Toad, to whom the realm was under tribute. He was a peevish and exacting monster from whom every one recoiled, and Ka Nam would have been terrified to approach him under ordinary conditions, but the peril which faced her gave her courage, and under the guidance of the mouse she went to the toad's cave.

KHASI PEASANTS.

When he saw her and beheld how fair she was, and learned how she had been the captive of his old rival the tiger, he readily consented to give her his protection; so he clothed her in a toadskin, warning her not to divest herself of it in the presence of others on pain of death. This he did in order to keep the maiden in his own custody and to make her his slave.

When the mouse saw that her beautiful friend had been transformed into the likeness of a hideous toad she was very sorrowful, and regretted having sent her to seek the protection of U Hynroh, for she knew that as long as she remained in the jungle Ka Nam would be henceforth forced to live with the toads and to be their slave. So she led her away secretly and brought her to the magic tree which was in that jungle, and told the maiden to climb into the tree that she might be transported to the sky, where she would be safe from harm for ever. So the maid climbed into the magic tree and spoke the magic words taught her by the mouse: "Grow tall, dear tree, the sky is near, expand and grow." Upon which the tree began to expand upwards till its branches touched the sky, and then the maiden alighted in the Blue Realm and the tree immediately dwindled to its former size.

By and by the tiger and his friends arrived at the den, ravenous for their feast, and when he found that his prey had disappeared his disappointment and anger knew no bounds and were terrible to witness. He uttered loud threats for vengeance on whoever had connived at the escape of his captive, and his roars were so loud that the animals in the jungle trembled with fear. His fellow-tigers also became enraged when they understood that they had been deprived of their feast, and they turned on U Khla and in their fury tore him to death.

Meanwhile Ka Nam wandered homeless in the Blue Realm, clothed in the toadskin. Every one there lived in palaces and splendour, and they refused to admit the loathsome, venomous-looking toad within their portals, while she, mindful of the warning of U Hynroh, the magician, feared to uncover herself. At last she appeared before the palace of Ka Sngi, the Sun, who, ever gracious and tender, took pity on her and permitted her to live in a small outhouse near the palace.

One day, thinking herself to be unobserved, the maid put aside her covering of toadskin and sat to rest awhile in her small room, but before going abroad she carefully wrapped herself in the skin as before. She was accidentally seen by the son of Ka Sngi, who was a very noble youth. He was astonished beyond words to find a maiden of such rare beauty hiding herself beneath a hideous toadskin and living in his mother's outhouse, and he marvelled what evil spell had caused her to assume such a loathsome covering. Her beauty enthralled him and he fell deeply in love with her.

He hastened to make his strange discovery known to his mother, and entreated her to lodge the maiden without delay in the palace and to let her become his wife. Ka Sngi, having the experience and foresight of age, determined to wait before acceding to the request of her young and impetuous son until she herself had ascertained whether a maid such as her son described really existed beneath the toadskin, or he had been deluded by some evil enchantment into imagining that he had seen a maiden in the outhouse.

So Ka Sngi set herself to watch the movements of

the toad in the outhouse, and one day, to her surprise and satisfaction, she beheld the maiden uncovered, and was astonished at her marvellous beauty and pleasing appearance. But she did not want her son to rush into an alliance with an enchanted maiden, so she gave him a command that he should not go near or speak to the maid until the toadskin had been destroyed and the evil spell upon her broken. Once again Ka Sngi set herself to watch the movements of the toad, and one day her vigilance was rewarded by discovering Ka Nam asleep with the toadskin cast aside. Ka Sngi crept stealthily and seized the toadskin and burned it to ashes. Henceforth the maiden appeared in her own natural form, and lived very happily as the wife of Ka Sngi's son, released for ever from the spell of the Giant Toad.

There was an old feud between U Hynroh and Ka Sngi because she refused to pay him tribute, and when he learned that she had wilfully destroyed the magic skin in which he had wrapped the maiden, his anger was kindled against Ka Sngi, and he climbed up to the Blue Realm to devour her. She bravely withstood him, and a fierce struggle ensued which was witnessed by the whole universe.

When mankind saw the conflict they became silent, subdued with apprehension lest the cruel monster should conquer their benefactress. They uttered loud cries and began to beat mournfully on their drums till the world was full of sound and clamour.

Like all bullies, U Hynroh was a real coward at heart, and when he heard the noise of drums and shouting on the earth, his heart melted within him with fear, for he thought it was the tramp of an advancing army coming to give him battle. He quickly released his hold upon

Ka Sngi and retreated with all speed from the Blue Realm. Thus mankind were the unconscious deliverers of their noble benefactress from the hand of her cruel oppressor.

U Hynroh continues to make periodical attacks on the sun to this day, and in many countries people call the attacks "Eclipses," but the Ancient Khasis, who saw the great conflict, knew it to be the Giant Toad, the great cannibal, trying to devour Ka Sngi. He endeavours to launch his attacks when the death of some great personage in the world is impending, hoping to catch mankind too preoccupied to come to the rescue. Throughout the whole of Khasi-land to this day it is the custom to beat drums and to raise a loud din whenever there is an eclipse.

II

THE LEGEND OF MOUNT SOPHET BNENG

SOPHET BNENG is a bare dome-like hill, about thirteen miles to the north of Shillong, and not far from the Shillong-Gauhati highroad to the East, from which it is plainly visible. Its name signifies the centre of heaven.

From the time of the creation of the world a tall tree, reaching to the sky, grew on the top of this hill, and was used by the heavenly beings as a ladder to ascend and descend between heaven and earth. At that time the earth was uninhabited, but all manner of trees and flowers grew in abundance, so that it was a very beautiful and desirable place, and they of heaven frequently came down to roam and to take their pleasure upon it.

When they found that the land in the neighbourhood of Sophet Bneng was fertile and goodly, they began to cultivate it for profit, but they never stayed overnight on the earth; they ascended to heaven, according to the decree. Altogether sixteen families followed the pastime of cultivating the land upon the earth.

Among the heavenly beings there was one who greatly coveted power, and was unwilling to remain the subject of his Creator, and aspired to rule over his brethren. He was constantly seeking for opportunities whereby to realise his ambitions.

One day it happened that seven families only of the cultivators chose to descend to the earth, the other nine remaining in heaven that day. When they were busy at work in their fields, the ambitious one covertly left his brethren, and, taking his axe secretly, he cut down the tree of communication, so that the seven families could not return to their heavenly home.

Thus it was that mankind came to live on the earth, and it is from these seven families—called by the Khasis "*Ki Hinniew Skum*" (the seven nests, or the seven roots)—who descended from heaven on that fatal day that all the nations of the earth have sprung.

III

HOW THE PEACOCK GOT HIS BEAUTIFUL FEATHERS

When the world was young and when all the animals spoke the language of mankind, the peacock, U Klew, was but an ordinary grey-feathered bird without any pretensions to beauty. But, even in those days, he was much given to pride and vanity, and strutted about with all the majesty of royalty, just because his tuft was more erect than the tuft of other birds and because his tail was longer and was carried with more grace than the tails of any of his companions.

He was a very unaccommodating neighbour. His tail was so big and unwieldy that he could not enter the houses of the more lowly birds, so he always attended the courts of the great, and was entertained by one or other of the wealthy birds at times of festivals in the jungle. This increased his high opinion of himself and added to his self-importance. He became so haughty and overbearing that he was cordially disliked by his neighbours, who endeavoured to repay him by playing many a jest at his expense.

They used to flatter him, pretending that they held him in very high esteem, simply for the amusement of seeing him swelling his chest and hearing him boast.

One day they pretended that a great Durbar of the birds had been held to select an ambassador to carry the greetings of the jungle birds to the beautiful maiden Ka Sngi, who ruled in the Blue Realm and poured her bright light so generously on their world, and that U Klew had been chosen for this great honour.

The peacock was very elated and became more swaggering than ever, and talked of his coming visit with great boastings, saying that not only was he going as the ambassador from the birds, but he was going in his own interests as well, and that he would woo and win the royal maiden for his wife and live with her in the Blue Realm.

The birds enjoyed much secret fun at his expense, none of them dreaming that he would be foolish enough to make the attempt to fly so far, for he was such a heavy-bodied bird and had never flown higher than a tree-top.

But much to the surprise of every one, the peacock expressed his intention of starting to the Blue Realm and bade his friends good-bye, they laughing among themselves, thinking how ridiculous he was making himself, and how angry he would be when he found how he had been duped. Contrary to their expectations, however, U Klew continued his flight upwards till they lost sight of him, and they marvelled and became afraid, not knowing to what danger their jest might drive him.

Strong on the wing, U Klew soared higher and higher, never halting till he reached the sky and alighted at the palace of Ka Sngi, the most beautiful of all maidens and the most good.

Now Ka Sngi was destined to live alone in her grand palace, and her heart often yearned for companionship.

When she saw that a stranger had alighted at her gates she rejoiced greatly, and hastened to receive him with courtesy and welcome. When she learned the errand upon which he had come, she was still happier, for she thought, "I shall never pine for companionship again, for this noble bird will always live with me"; and she smiled upon the world and was glad.

When U Klew left the earth and entered the realm of light and sunshine, he did not cast from him his selfish and conceited nature, but rather his selfishness and conceit grew more pronounced as his comforts and luxuries increased. Seeing the eager welcome extended to him by the beautiful maiden, he became more uplifted and exacting than ever and demanded all sorts of services at her hands; he grew surly and cross unless she was always in attendance upon him. Ka Sngi, on the other hand, was noble and generous and delighted to render kindnesses to others. She loved to shine upon the world and to see it responding to her warmth and her smiles. To her mate, U Klew, she gave unstinted attention and waited upon him with unparalleled love and devotion, which he received with cold indifference, considering that all this attention was due to his own personal greatness, rather than to the gracious and unselfish devotion of his consort.

In former times Ka Sngi had found one of the chief outlets for her munificence in shedding her warm rays upon the earth; but after the coming of U Klew her time became so absorbed by him that she was no longer able to leave her palace, so the earth became cold and dreary, and the birds in the jungle became cheerless, their feathers drooped, and their songs ceased. U Slap, the rain, came and pelted their cosy nests without mercy, causing their young ones to die; U Lyoh, the mist, brought his dark clouds and hung them over the rice fields so that no grain ripened; and Ka Eriong, the storm, shook the trees, destroying all the fruit, so that the birds wandered about homeless and without food.

In their great misery they sought counsel of mankind, whom they knew to be wiser than any of the animals. By means of divinations mankind ascertained that all these misfortunes were due to the presence of U Klew in the Blue Realm, for his selfish disposition prevented Ka Sngi from bestowing her light and her smiles upon the world as in former times; and there was no hope for prosperity until U Klew could be lured back to jungle-land.

In those days there lived in the jungle a cunning woman whose name was Ka Sabuit. Acting on the advice of mankind, the birds invoked her aid to encompass the return of the peacock from the Blue Realm. At that time Ka Sabuit was very destitute, owing to the great famine; she had nothing to eat except some wild roots and no seed to sow in her garden except one gourdful of mustard seeds—the cheapest and most common of all seeds—and even this she was afraid to sow lest the hungry birds should come and devour it and leave her without a grain.

When the birds came to seek counsel of her she was very pleased, hoping that she could by some design force them to promise not to rob her garden. After they had explained to her their trouble, she undertook to bring U Klew back to the jungle within thirteen moons on two conditions: one, that the birds should refrain from picking the seeds from her garden; the other, that they should torment the animals if they came to eat her crops or to trample on her land. These appeared such easy terms that the birds readily agreed to them.

The garden of the cunning woman was in an open part of the jungle and could be seen from many of the hill-tops around, and in past days the sun used to shine upon it from morning till night. Thither Ka Sabuit wended her way after the interview with the birds, and she began to dig the ground with great care and patience, bestowing much more time upon it than she had ever been known to do. Her neighbours laughed and playfully asked her if she expected a crop of precious stones to grow from her mustard seed that year that she spent so much labour upon the garden, but the elderly dame took no heed. She worked on patiently and kept her own counsel while the birds waited and watched.

She shaped her mustard bed like unto the form of a woman; this provoked the mirth of her neighbours still more and incited many questions from them, but Ka Sabuit took no heed. She worked patiently on and kept her own counsel while the birds waited and watched.

By and by the seeds sprouted; and the plot of land shaped like a woman became covered with glistening green leaves, while the birds continued to watch and to keep the animals at bay, and the cunning woman watered and tended her garden, keeping her own counsel.

In time small yellow flowers appeared on all the mustard plants, so that the plot of land shaped like a woman looked in the distance like a beautiful maiden wearing a mantle of gold that dazzled the eyes. When the neighbours saw it they wondered at the beauty of it and admired the skill of the cunning woman; but no one could understand or guess at her reason for the strange freak and Ka Sabuit threw no light on the matter. She still patiently worked on and kept her own counsel.

Up in the Blue Realm U Klew continued his despotic and arrogant sway, while his gentle and noble wife spared no pains to gratify his every wish. Like all pampered people who are given all their desires, the peacock became fretful and more and more difficult to please, tiring of every diversion, and ever seeking some new source of indulgence, till at last nothing seemed to satisfy him; even the splendours and magnificence of the palace of Ka Sngi began to pall.

Now and then memories of his old home and old associates came to disturb his mind, and he often wondered to himself what had been the fate of his old playmates in jungle-land. One day he wandered forth from the precincts of the palace to view his old haunts, and as he recognised one familiar landmark after another his eye was suddenly arrested by the sight of (as it seemed to him) a lovely maiden dressed all in gold lying asleep in a garden in the middle of the forest where he himself had once lived. At sight of her his heart melted like water within him for the love of her. He forgot the allegiance due to his beautiful and high-born wife, Ka Sngi; he could only think of the maiden dressed all in gold, lying asleep in a jungle garden, guarded by all the birds.

After this U Klew was reluctant to remain in the Blue Realm. His whole being yearned for the maiden he had seen lying asleep on the earth, and one day, to his wife's sorrow, he communicated his determination to return to his native land to seek the object of his new love. Ka Sngi became a sorrowful wife, for there is no pang so piercing to the heart of a constant woman as the pang inflicted by being forsaken by her husband. With all manner of inducements and persuasions and charms she tried to prevail upon him to keep faithful to his marriage vows, but he was heartless and obdurate; and, unmindful of all ties, he took his departure. As he went away Ka Sngi followed him, weeping, and as she wept her tears bedewed his feathers, transforming them into all the colours of the rainbow. Some large drops falling on his long tail as he flew away were turned into brilliant-hued spots, which are called "*Ummat Ka Sngi*" (the Sun's tears) by the Khasis to this day. Ka Sngi told him that they were given for a sign that wherever he might be and on whomsoever his affections might be bestowed, he would never be able to forget her, Ka Sngi, the most beautiful and the most devoted of wives.

Thus U Klew, the peacock, came back to the jungle. The birds, when they saw his beautiful feathers, greeted him with wonder and admiration. When he informed them that he had come in quest of a lovely maiden dressed all in gold, they began to laugh, and it now became clear to them what had been the object of the cunning woman when she shaped her mustard bed like unto the shape of a woman. They invited U Klew to come and be introduced to the object of his love, and they led him forth with great ceremony to the garden of Ka Sabuit, where he beheld, not a beautiful maiden as he had imagined, but a bed of common mustard cunningly shaped. His shame and humiliation were pitiful to behold; he tried to fly back to the Blue Realm, but he was no longer able to take a long flight; so, uttering the most sad and plaintive cries, he had to resign himself to the life of the jungle for ever.

Every morning, it is said, the peacock can be seen stretching forth his neck towards the sky and flapping his wings to greet the coming of Ka Sngi; and the only happiness left to him is to spread his lovely feathers to catch the beams which she once more sheds upon the earth.

IV

THE GODDESS WHO CAME TO LIVE WITH MANKIND

(A Legend of the Shillong Peak)

Shillong Peak is the highest mountain in the Khasi Hills, and although it bears such a prosaic name in our days, the mountain was a place of renown in the days of the Ancient Khasis, full of romance and mystery, sacred to the spirits and to the gods. In those days the mountain itself, and the whole country to the north of it, was one vast forest, where dwelt demons and dragons, who cast evil spells and caused dire sickness to fall upon any unfortunate person who happened to spend a night in that wild forest.

In the mountain there lived a god. At first the Ancients had no clear revelation about this deity ; they were vaguely aware of his existence, but there was no decree that sacrifices should be offered to him. After a time there arose among the Khasis a very wise man of the name of U Shillong who was endowed with great insight to understand the mysteries, and he discovered that the god of the mountain was great and powerful, and sacrifice and reverence should be offered to him, and he taught his neighbours how to perform the rites acceptably. The name of the deity was not revealed, so the people began to call him "U 'Lei Shillong" (the god of U Shillong) after the name of the man who first paid him homage. Then gradually he came to be called "the god Shillong," and in time the mountain itself was called the mountain of Shillong, and from this is derived the name of the present town of Shillong.

AT THE FOOT OF MOUNT SHILLONG.

Possibly the god Shillong was, and remains, one of the best-known and most generally reverenced of all the Khasi gods, for even on the far hill-tops of Jaintia altars have been raised to his service and honour. Although sacrifices are being offered to him at distant shrines, the abode of the god is in the Shillong mountain, more especially in the sacred grove on the summit of the peak itself, which is such a familiar landmark in the country.

Judging from tradition, this deity was regarded as a benign and benevolent being, forbearing in his attitude towards mankind, who were privileged to hunt in his forests unhindered by dangers and sicknesses, and the dances of mankind were acceptable in his sight. He frequently assisted them in their misfortunes and helped them to overcome the oppression of demons. It was he who endowed U Suidnoh with wisdom to fight and to conquer U Thlen, the great snake-god and vampire from Cherrapoonjee, and it was by his intervention that Ka Thei and her sister were delivered from the grasp of the merciless demon, U Ksuid Tynjang.

Tradition also points out that this famous deity had a wife and family, and three at least of his daughters are renowned in Khasi folk-lore. One of them transformed herself into the likeness of a Khasi maiden and came to live with mankind, where she became the ancestress of a race of chiefs. Two other daughters, out of playfulness, transformed themselves into two rivers, and are with us in that form to this day. This is the story of the goddess who came to live with mankind:

Many hundreds of years ago, near the place now known as Pomlakrai, there was a cave called the Cave of Marai, near to which stood a high perpendicular rock around which the youthful cow-herds of the time used to play. They gathered there from different directions, and passed the time merrily, practising archery and playing on their flutes, while keeping an eye on their herds. The rock was too high for them to attempt to climb it, and it was always spoken of as "the rock on which the foot of man never trod."

On a certain day, when the lads came as usual to the familiar rendezvous, they were surprised to see, sitting on the top of the rock, a fair young girl watching them silently and wistfully. The children, being superstitious, took fright at sight of her and ran in terror to Mylliem, their village, leaving the cattle to shift for themselves. When they told their news, the whole village was roused and men quickly gathered to the public meeting-place to hold a consultation. They decided to go and see for themselves if the apparition seen by the children was a real live child, or if they had been deluded by some spell or enchantment. Under the guidance of the lads, they hurried to the place on the hill where the rock stood, and there, as the boys had stated, sat a fair and beautiful child.

The clothes worn by the little girl were far richer than any worn by their own women-folk, so they judged that she belonged to some rich family, and she was altogether so lovely that the men gazed open-mouthed at her, dazzled by her beauty. Their sense of chivalry soon asserted itself, however, and they began to devise plans to rescue the maiden from her perilous position. To climb up the face of that steep rock was an impossible feat; so they called to her, but she would not answer; they made signs for her to descend, but she did not stir, and the men felt baffled and perplexed.

Chief among the rescuers was a man called U Mylliem Ngap, who was remarkable for his sagacity and courage. When he saw that the child refused to be coaxed, he attributed it to her fear to venture unaided down that steep and slippery rock. So he sent some of his comrades to the jungle to cut down some bamboos, which he joined together and made into a pole long enough to reach the top of the rock. Then he beckoned to the child to take hold of it, but she sat on unmoved.

By this time the day was beginning to wane, yet the child did not stir and the rescuers were growing desperate. To leave her to her fate on that impregnable rock would be little less than cold-blooded murder, for nothing but death awaited her. They began to lament loudly, as people lament when mourning for their dead, but the child sat on in the same indifferent attitude.

Just then U Mylliem Ngap noticed a tuft of wild flowers growing near the cave, and he quickly gathered a bunch and fastened it to the end of the long pole and held it up to the maiden's view. The moment she saw the flowers, she gave a cry of delight and held out her hand to take them. U Mylliem Ngap promptly lowered the pole and the child moved towards it, but before she could grasp the flowers the pole was again lowered; so, little by little, step by step, as the men watched with bated breath, the little maid reached the ground in safety.

U Mylliem Ngap, with general consent, constituted himself her champion. He called her "Pah Syntiew," which means "Lured by Flowers," for her name and her origin were unknown. He took her to his own home and adopted her as his own daughter, cherishing her with fondness and affection, which the child fully requited.

Ka Pah Syntiew, as she grew up, fulfilled all the promises of her childhood and developed into a woman of incomparable beauty and her fame went abroad throughout the country. She was also gifted and wise beyond all the maidens of the neighbourhood, and was the chosen leader at all the Khasi dances and festivals. She taught the Khasi girls to dance and to sing, and it was she who instituted the Virgins' Dance, which remains popular to this day among the Khasis. Her foster-father, seeing she possessed so much discretion and wisdom, used to consult her in all his perplexities and seek her advice in all matters pertaining to the ruling of the village. She displayed such tact and judgement that people from other villages brought their disputes to her to be settled, and she was acknowledged to be wiser and more just than any ruler in the country, and they began to call her "Ka Siem" (the Chiefess, or the Queen).

When she came of age, U Mylliem Ngap gave her in marriage to a man of prowess and worth, who is mentioned in Khasi lore as "U Kongor Nongjri." She became the mother of many sons and daughters, who were all noble and comely.

After her children had grown up, Ka Pah Syntiew called them all to her one day and revealed to them the secret of her birth. She was the daughter of U 'Lei Shillong, the mountain god, permitted by her father to dwell for a period among mankind, and at last the time was at hand for her to return to her native element.

Not long after this Ka Pah Syntiew walked away in the direction of the cave of Marai, and no one dared to accompany her, for it was realised that her hour of departure had come. From that day she disappeared from mortal ken. Her descendants are known to this day as two of the leading families of Khasi chiefs, or Siems, and in common parlance these two families, those of Khairim and Mylliem, are still called "the Siems (the Chiefs) of Shillong," or "the Siems of the god."

V

THE FORMATION OF THE EARTH

When the earth was created, it was one great plain. full of vast forests and smooth rivers. Then it happened that the mother of the three goddesses, Ka Ding, Ka Um, and Ka Sngi, died while wandering abroad one day on the earth. These goddesses are Fire, Water, and the Sun. It became necessary for the daughters to discover some means whereby their mother's body could be put away out of their sight and not be left exposed on the face of the earth.

According to the decree, it was decided that Ka Sngi, being the youngest, should perform the rites of destroying the body; so Ka Sngi went out in all her strength, and put forth great heat till the rivers were dried up and all the leaves of the forest and the grass withered, but the body of the mother was not consumed. So Ka Sngi returned to her sisters and said, "I have exhausted all my powers, but our mother's body still lies on the face of the earth in our sight."

After this the next sister, Ka Um, undertook to perform the rites, and she went forth with a great company of clouds, and poured incessant rain upon the earth till the rivers and pools were all flooded, but her mother's body was not destroyed. So Ka Um also returned to her sisters and said, "I have exhausted all my powers, but the body of our mother still lies on the face of the earth in our sight."

Thus it remained for the elder sister, Ka Ding, to undertake to do the necessary rites, and she spread forth great flames which swept over the forests and caused the earth to burn and to crumble till the vast plain lost its contour and the body of the mother was consumed.

Ever since then the earth has remained as the fire left it, full of mountains and valleys and gorges. It became a much more beautiful place, and in time mankind came here from heaven to dwell.

VI

THE LEGEND OF U RAITONG, THE KHASI ORPHEUS

A FEW miles to the north of Shillong, the chief town of the Province of Assam, there is a fertile and pleasant hill known as the Hill of Raitong, which is one of the most famous spots in ancient folk-lore, and for which is claimed the distinction of being the place where the custom of suttee—wife-sacrifice of the Hindus—originated. The legend runs as follows:

Many ages ago there lived a great Siem (Chief) who ruled over large territories and whose sceptre swayed many tribes and clans of people. As befitted such a great Siem, his consort, the Mahadei, was a woman of great beauty: her figure was erect and lissom and all her movements easy and graceful as the motion of the palms in the summer breeze; her hair was long and flowing, enfolding her like a wreathing cloud; her teeth were even as the rims of a cowrie; her lips were red as the precious coral and fragrant as the flower of Lasubon; and her face was fair like unto the face of a goddess. Strange to relate, the names of this famous royal couple have not been transmitted to posterity.

It came to pass that affairs of the State necessitated the absence of the Siem from home for a protracted period. He appointed deputies to govern the village and to control his household during the interval, while the Mahadei, who was unto him as the apple of his eye, was placed under the joint guardianship of her own and his own family. When he had made all satisfactory arrangements he took his departure and went on his long journey accompanied by the good wishes of his people.

Among the subjects of the Siem was a poor beggar lad, who was looked upon as being half-witted, for he spent his days roaming about the village clothed in filthy rags, his head and face covered with ashes like a wandering fakir. He never conversed with any of the villagers, but kept muttering to himself incessantly, lamenting his own forlorn and friendless condition.

His name was U Raitong. Formerly he had been a happy and well-cared-for lad, surrounded and loved by many relatives and kindred, until a terrible epidemic swept through the village and carried away all his family and left him orphaned and alone, without sustenance and without a relative to stand by his bedside in time of sickness or to perform the funeral rites over his body when he died. Overwhelmed by grief and sorrow, U Raitong vowed a rash vow that all the days of his life should be spent in mourning the death of his kindred ; thus it was that he walked about the village lamenting to himself and wearing ragged clothes. His neighbours, not knowing about the vow, thought that sorrow had turned his head, so they treated him as an idiot and pitied him and gave him alms.

His condition was so wretched and his clothes so tattered that he became a proverb in the country, and to this day, when the Khasis wish to describe one fallen into extreme poverty and wretchedness, they say, "as poor as U Raitong."

At night time, however, U Raitong considered himself free from the obligations of his rash vow, and when he retired to his rickety cabin on the outskirts of the village he divested himself of his rags and arrayed himself in fine garments, and would play for hours on his sharati (flute), a bamboo instrument much in vogue among the Khasis to this day. He was a born musician, and constant practice had made him an accomplished player, and never did flute give forth sweeter and richer music than did the sharati of U Raitong as he played by stealth in the hours of the night when all the village was asleep.

The melodies he composed were so enthralling that he often became oblivious to all his surroundings and abandoned himself to the charms of his own subtle music. His body swayed and trembled with pure joy and delight as he gave forth strain after strain from his sharati; yet so cautious was he that none of his neighbours suspected that he possessed any gifts, for he feared to let it be known lest it should interfere with the performance of his vow.

It happened one night that the Mahadei was restless and unable to sleep, and as she lay awake she heard the faint strains of the most sweet music wafted on the air. She imagined that it was coming from the fairies who were said to inhabit certain parts of the forest, and she listened enraptured until the sounds ceased. When it stopped, a feeling of great loneliness came over her, so overawing that she could not summon enough courage to speak about the strange music she had heard. She went about her household duties with her thoughts far away and longing for the night to come in the hope that the music would be wafted to her again.

The following night, and for many successive nights, the Mahadei lay awake to listen, and was always rewarded by hearing the soft sweet strains of some musical instrument floating on the air till she imagined the room to be full of some beautiful beings singing the sweetest melodies that human ears ever heard. When it ceased, as it always did before daybreak, the feeling of desolation was intense, till her whole mind became absorbed with thoughts of the mysterious music.

The fascination grew until at last it became overpowering and she could no longer resist the desire to know whence the sounds proceeded. She crept stealthily from her room one night, and following the direction of the strains, she walked through the village and was surprised to find that the music emerged from the dilapidated hut of U Raitong.

The heart of the Mahadei was touched, for she thought that the fairies in tenderness and pity came to cheer and to comfort the poor idiot with their music, and she stood there to listen. The strains which she could hear but faintly in her own room now broke upon her in all their fulness and richness till her whole being was ravished by them.

Before dawn the sounds suddenly ceased, and the Mahadei retraced her steps stealthily and crept back to her room without being observed by any one. After this she stole out of her house every night and went to listen to what she believed to be fairy-music outside the hut of U Raitong.

One night, when the power of the music was stronger than usual, the Mahadei drew near and peeped through a crevice in the door, and to her astonishment, instead of the fairies she had pictured, she saw that it was U Raitong, the supposed idiot, who was playing on his sharati, but a Raitong so changed from the one she had been accustomed to see about the village that she could scarcely believe her own eyes. He was well and tastefully dressed and his face was alight with joy, while his body moved with graceful motions as he swayed with rapture in harmony with the rhythm of his wild music. She stood spellbound, as much moved by the sight that met her eyes as she had been by the charm of the music, and, forgetful of her marriage vows and her duty to her absent husband, she fell deeply and irrevocably in love with U Raitong.

Time passed, and the Mahadei continued to visit the hut of U Raitong by stealth, drawn by her passionate love for him even more than by the fascination of his sharati. At first U Raitong was unaware that he was being spied upon, but when he discovered the Mahadei in his hut, he was greatly troubled, and tried to reason with her against coming with as much sternness as was becoming in one of his class to show to one so much above him in rank. But she overruled all his scruples, and before long the intensity of her love for him and the beauty of her person awoke similar feelings in him and he fell a victim to her wicked and unbridled passion.

The months rolled on and the time for the return of the Siem was advancing apace. People began to discuss the preparations for celebrating his return, and every one evinced the most lively interest except the Mahadei. It was noticed that she, the most interested person of all, appeared the most unconcerned, and people marvelled to see her so cold and indifferent; but one day the reason became clear when it was announced that a son had been born to the Mahadei and that her guardians had locked her up in one of the rooms of the court, pending the arrival of the Siem. She offered no resistance and put forward no justification, but when questioned as to the identity of her child's father she remained resolutely silent.

When the Siem arrived and heard of his wife's infidelity he was bowed down with shame and grief, and vowed that he would enforce the extreme penalty of the law on the man who had sullied her honour, but neither persuasion nor coercion could extract from the Mahadei his name.

It was necessary for the well-being of the State, as well as for the satisfaction of the Siem, that the culprit should be found; so the Siem sent a mandate throughout his territory calling upon all the male population, on penalty of death, to attend a great State Durbar, when the Siem and his ministers would sit in judgement to discover the father of the child of the faithless Mahadei.

Never in the history of Durbars was seen such a multitude gathered together as was seen on that day when all the men, both young and old, appeared before the Siem to pass through the test laid down by him. When all had assembled, the Siem ordered a mat to be brought and placed in the centre, and the babe laid upon it; after which he commanded every man to walk round the mat in procession and, as he passed, to offer a plantain to the child, inasmuch as it was believed that the instincts of the babe would lead him to accept a plantain from the hand of his own father and from no other.

The long procession filed past one by one, but the babe gave no sign, and the Siem and his ministers were baffled and perplexed. They demanded to know what man had absented himself, but when the roll was called the number was complete. Some one in the throng shouted the name of U Raitong, at which many laughed, for no one deemed him to be sane; other voices said mockingly, "Send for him"; others said, "Why trouble about such a witless creature? He is but as a dog or a rat." Thus the Durbar was divided, but the ministers, unwilling to pass over even the most hapless, decided to send for him and to put him through the test like the other men.

When the Siem's messengers arrived at the hut they found U Raitong just as usual, dressed in filthy rags and muttering to himself, his face covered with ashes. He arose immediately and followed the men to the place of Durbar, and as he came people pitied him, for he looked so sad and forlorn and defenceless that it seemed a shame to put such an one through the test. A plantain was put into his hand and he was told to walk past the mat. As soon as the babe saw him he began to crow with delight and held out his hands for the plantain, but he took no notice of the well-dressed people who crowded round.

There was a loud commotion when the secret was discovered, and the Siem looked ashamed and humiliated to find that one so unseemly and poor was proved to be the lover of his beautiful wife. The assembly were awed at the spectacle, and many of them raised their voices in thanksgiving to the deity whom they considered to have directed the course of events and brought the guilty to judgement.

The Siem commanded his ministers to pronounce judgement, and they with one accord proclaimed that he should be burned to death, without the performance of any rites and that no hand should gather his bones for burial. In this decision all the throng acquiesced, for such was the law and the decree.

U Raitong received the verdict with indifference as one who had long known and become reconciled to his fate, but he asked one boon, and that was permission to build his own pyre and play a dirge for himself. The Siem and the people were astonished to hear him speak in clear tones instead of the blubbering manner in which he had always been known to speak. Nobody raised an objection to his request, so he received permission to build his own pyre and to play his own dirge.

Accordingly on the morrow U Raitong arose early and gathered a great pile of dry firewood and laid it carefully till the pyre was larger than the pyres built for the cremation of Siems and the great ones of the land. After finishing the pyre he returned to his lonely hut and divested himself of his filthy rags and arrayed himself in the fine garments which he used to wear in the hours of the night when he abandoned himself to music; he then took his sharati in his hand and sallied forth to his terrible doom. As he marched towards the pyre he played on his sharati, and the sound of his dirge was carried by the air to every dwelling in the village, and so beautiful was it and so enchanting, so full of wild pathos and woe, that it stirred every heart. People flocked after him, wondering at the changed appearance of U Raitong and fascinated by the marvellous and mysterious music such as they had never before heard, which arrested and charmed every ear.

When the procession reached the pyre, U Raitong stooped and lighted the dry logs without a shudder or a delay. Then once more he began to play on his sharati and marched three times round the pyre, and as he marched he played such doleful and mournful melodies that his hearers raised their voices in a loud wail in sympathy, so that the wailing and the mourning at the pyre of the unfortunate U Raitong was more sincere and impressive than the mourning made for the greatest men in the country.

At the end of his third round U Raitong suddenly stopped his music, planted his sharati point downward in the earth, and leaped upon the burning pyre and perished.

While these events were taking place outside, the Mahadei remained a close prisoner in her room, and no whisper of what was transpiring was allowed to reach her. But her heart was heavy with apprehension for her lover, and when she heard the notes of a sharati she knew it could be none other than U Raitong, and that the secret had been discovered and that he was being sent to his doom.

As before, the notes of the sharati seemed to call her irresistibly, and with almost superhuman strength she burst open the door of her prison. Great as was her excitement and her desire to get away, she took precautions to cover her escape. Seeing a string of cowries with which her child had been playing, she hastily fastened them to the feet of a kitten that was in the room, so that whenever the kitten moved the noise of the cowries jingling on the floor of the room would lead those outside to think that it was the Mahadei herself still moving about; then she sped forth to the hill in the direction of the sound of the sharati and the wailing. When she arrived at the pyre, U Raitong had just taken his fatal leap. She pushed her way resolutely through the dense and wailing crowd, and before any one could anticipate her action she too had leaped into the flaming furnace to die by the side of her lover.

The Siem alone of all the people in the village had withstood the fascination of the dirge. He sat in his chamber morose and outraged, brooding on his calamity. Just when the Mahadei was leaping into the flames a strange thing happened in the Siem's chamber—the head-cloth (*tapmoh*) of his wife was blown in a mysterious manner so that it fell at his feet although there was not enough breeze to cause a leaf to rustle. When the Siem saw it he said, "By this token my wife must be dead." Still hearing sounds coming from her room, he tried to take no heed of the omen. The foreboding, however, grew so strong that he got up to investigate, and when he opened the door of the room where the Mahadei had been imprisoned he found it empty, save for a kitten with a string of cowries fastened to its feet.

He knew instinctively whither she had gone, and in the hope of averting further scandal he hurried in her wake towards the pyre on the hill, but he was too late. When he arrived on the scene he found only her charred remains.

The news of the unparalleled devotion of the Mahadei to her lover spread abroad throughout the land and stirred the minds of men and women in all countries. The chaste wives of India, when they heard of it, said one to another, "We must not allow the unholy passion of an unchaste woman to become more famous than the sacred love of holy matrimony. Henceforth we will offer our bodies on the altar of death, on the pyre of our husbands, to prove our devotion and fidelity." Thus originated the custom of suttee (wife-sacrifice) in many parts of India.

The Khasis were so impressed by the suitability of the sharati to express sorrow and grief that they have adopted that instrument ever since to play their dirges at times of cremation.

The sharati of U Raitong, which he planted in the earth as he was about to leap to his doom, took root, and a clump of bamboos grew from it, distinguishable from all other bamboos by having their branches forking downwards. It is commonly maintained to this day that there are clumps of bamboos forking downwards to be found in plenty on the Hill of Raitong.

VII

THE TIGER AND THE MONKEYS

At the beginning of time the animals were free and living wild and unruly lives, but there were so many disputes and quarrels that they convened a council to choose a king to reign over them. With one accord they nominated the tiger to be king, not for any special wisdom or merit which he possessed, but because of his great strength, by which he would be able to subdue the turbulent beasts.

Although he possessed greater strength than any of his kindred, the tiger was more ignorant of the ways and habits of his subjects than any of the animals. He was so self-absorbed that he never troubled himself to study the ways of others, and this caused him to act very foolishly at times and to make himself ridiculous, for the animals were tempted to take advantage of his great ignorance and to play tricks upon him whenever they thought they could do so undetected. This tale relates how the monkeys played a cunning trick on their king which caused mortal enmity to spring up between him and them for ever.

One hot day the tiger walked abroad to take an airing, but, the sun being so hot, he turned aside to shelter under some leafy trees and there he fell asleep.

Presently he awoke, and on awaking he heard coming from overhead very melodious singing to which he listened enraptured. It was the little insect, Shalymmen, chirping on a leaf, but she was so small the tiger could not see her, and, being so ignorant, he had no idea whose voice it was. He peered to the branches right and left trying to discover the singer, but he only saw a company of monkeys at play in the trees, so he began to question them who it was that was singing above him.

Now the monkeys and all the jungle animals were perfectly familiar with the singing of Shalymmen and recognised the voice from afar. They thought it very contemptible in the king to be more ignorant than themselves, and one audacious young monkey, in a spirit of mischief, answered that the singer was their youngest sister.

The other monkeys were perturbed when they heard their brother giving such an impudent answer, thinking that the tiger would be offended and would punish them with his great strength. They were preparing to run away when, to their amazement, they heard the tiger replying to their rash young brother in a gentle voice and with most affable manners and saying to him, "You are my brother-in-law. Your sister has the most beautiful voice in the jungle; I will make her my wife."

If the predicament of the monkeys was bad at the beginning, it was doubly so now, for they felt that, things having taken such an unexpected turn, it would be impossible to conceal from the knowledge of the tiger their brother's offence. They determined, however, not to desert the young culprit, and if possible to try and rescue him, so they approached the tiger, and with much seeming courtesy and honour they put forward the excuse that their sister was very young and not yet of marriageable age. This excuse made no impression on the king, for he said:

"So much the better. As she is young, I can mould her to my own ways, and bring her up according to my own views, which would not be so easy if she were fully matured."

To which the monkeys replied, "Our sister is not amenable to instruction. She is indolent and fond of her own will."

The tiger, however, was so lovesick that no argument had weight with him. He thought the brothers were severe in their judgement, and expressed his conviction that she could not be as slothful as they said, for she was forgoing her midday repose for the sake of making music to cheer the animals. He ordered them to come down from the trees and to lead their sister to him.

After this the monkeys feared to argue further, so they pretended to agree to his commands; but they craved a boon from him, and asked for a little time to make preparations, as it would not be becoming for one of such a high degree to join himself with a poor family like theirs without their showing him adequate honour such as was due to his rank. This request the tiger granted, and it was arranged between them that he was to come and claim his bride at the time of the full moon, a week from that day, and so the tiger departed with evident goodwill.

As soon as they found themselves alone the monkeys began to think out some plans by which they could meet the situation and escape exposure. They decided to call together a council of the whole tribe of monkeys, for they well foresaw that the whole tribe would be in peril if the tiger found out what they had done. So the monkeys came to hold a council, and in that council it was decided that they must continue to keep up the duplicity begun, and in order to hoodwink the tiger still further they planned to make a clay image after the fashion of a woman and to present her to the tiger as his bride. So they made preparations for a great feast, but they did not invite anybody except their own tribe to attend.

During the succeeding days the monkeys busied themselves collecting clay and moulding it into an image, which they propped against a tree. They were unable to make the head of one piece with the body, so they moulded the head separately, and when it was finished they placed it loosely on the body of the image. They then proceeded to dress the image in all the finery they could procure, and they carefully covered the head and face with a veil so as to hide it from the eyes of the bridegroom.

The night of the full moon arrived, and all the monkey family were assembled at the appointed place, where with much clatter and seeming joy they awaited the arrival of the tiger, though they were really very anxious about the consequences. Everything was in readiness, and the place laid out with many kinds of food, so as to lead the tiger to think that they were sincere in their welcome.

He came early, very gorgeously arrayed, and carrying over his shoulder a net full of betel nut and pan leaves, and was received with loud acclamation by his prospective relatives. But the tiger hardly deigned to give them a greeting, so impatient was he to meet his bride, and he demanded to be taken to her immediately. The monkeys led him with great ceremony to the clay image, but their hearts were beating fast with fear lest he should discover their fraud.

When they reached the image they said, "This is our sister. Take her and may she be worthy of the great honour you have conferred upon her." Thereupon they retired to a safe distance.

When the tiger saw how finely dressed she was and how modestly she had veiled herself, he felt a little timid, for she was so much finer than the little grey monkey he had been picturing to himself. He came up to her and said deferentially, as he slung the net of betel nut round her neck:

"You are the chief person at this feast, take the pan and the betel nut and divide them among the company according to custom."

The bride, however, remained motionless and mute, seeing which, the tiger asked the monkeys in a displeased voice, "Why doth not your sister answer me nor obey my commands?"

"She is very young," they replied, "perhaps she has fallen asleep while waiting for you; pull the string of the net and she will awaken."

Upon this the tiger gave the string a sharp tug, and the loose head of the image rolled on to the floor, whereupon the monkeys, uttering the most piercing shrieks, pounced upon the tiger in a mob, declaring that he had killed their sister, and that he had only made a pretence of marrying her in order to get hold of her to kill her. A fierce and bloody fight ensued in which the tiger was nearly killed, and ever since then the tiger has feared the monkeys, and they are the only animals in the jungle that dare challenge him to fight. He never discovered their duplicity, but he learned one very effective lesson, for he has never committed the indiscretion of proposing marriage with an unknown bride since that unfortunate affair with the monkeys; while the monkeys are rejoicing in the cunning by which they saved their brother and their tribe from punishment.

VIII

THE LEGEND OF THE IEI TREE

Some eight or ten miles to the west of the town of Shillong is seen a prominent hill range, a place much renowned in Khasi folk-lore. It is known as the Mountain of the Iei Tree, and is a very romantic spot even in the present day, although divested of its former reputed glory. Its slopes are studded with thriving villages and cultivated fields, which appear from a distance like a bit of British landscape. At its foot the river Umiam (the wailing river) curves its dolorous way to the plains, at times leaping wildly over rugged precipices, scattering its spray in the sunshine, at other times lying almost motionless in the bosom of a valley, reflecting the beauty of myriad trees in its clear depths.

According to tradition, this hill, and the land around it, was the most fertile land in the world; broad acres lay under cultivation and its forests yielded the largest and most valuable timber. It was also famous for the grandeur of its scenery; fairies and nymphs were said to have their haunts in its green glades, birds of lovely hues lived there and made their nests amid flowers of sweetest scent; there happy maidens loved to roam, and there young lovers met and plighted their troth.

Such was the Mountain of the Iei Tree in the days of the Ancients.

On the summit of the mountain there grew a tree of fabulous dimensions—the Iei Tree—which dwarfed even the largest trees in forests. It was of a species unique, such as mankind had never known; its thick outspreading branches were so clustered with leaves that

AT THE FOOT OF THE MOUNTAIN OF THE IEI TREE.

the light of the sun could not penetrate through and the earth beneath its shadow became barren and unfruitful.

The fame of the tree spread abroad and people from many lands came to see it, but there were none who dared to cut a twig or to scratch its bark, as it was commonly believed that the tree was the abode of some unknown and powerful god, to offend whom would bring destruction.

The Iei Tree continued to grow through many ages, and year by year its malevolent shadow spread further

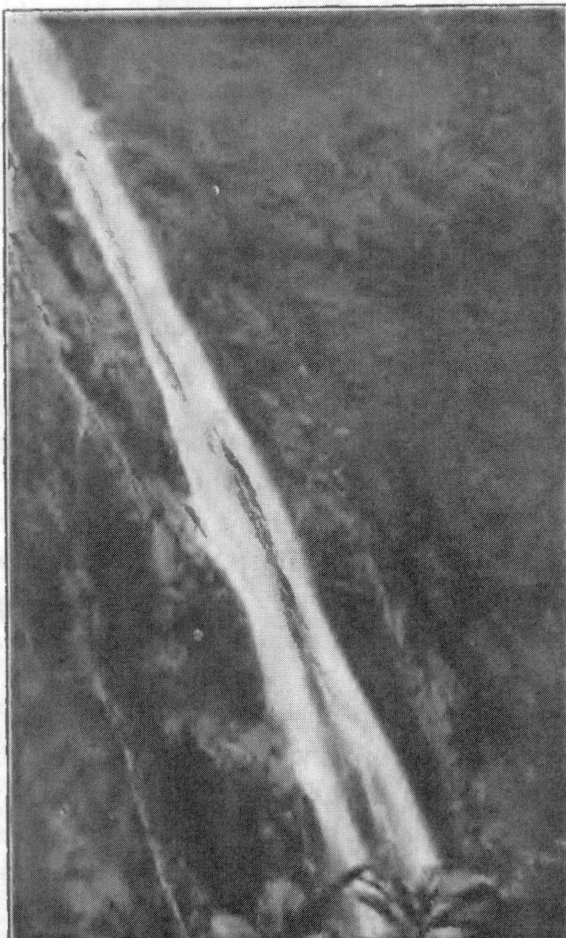

A KHASI WATERFALL IN THE NEIGHBOURHOOD OF THE MOUNTAIN OF THE IEI TREE.

and further, and the area of the barren land increased season by season until at last it became a serious menace to the world, and the very existence of mankind was at stake. People could no longer live on the slopes of the mountain, cultivation became impossible for many miles around, and the one-time prosperous families had to wander abroad as homeless fugitives, fleeing from the ever-pursuing, ever-threatening shadow. The pathways and pleasant nooks whence of old had echoed the merry voices and laughter of children were now become the lurking-places of dragons and the prowling-grounds of savage beasts whither no man ventured to roam.

A Durbar of all mankind was summoned to consider the situation and to devise some plan to save the world from its impending doom. After long and solemn deliberations, it was resolved to mobilise a party of the bravest and most skilled wood-cutters to go into the mountain to hew down the Iei Tree so as to admit the sunlight once more to the earth. In the course of time the wood-cutters came and entered the mountain, defying all danger and risking the possible wrath of the unknown god whom they believed to haunt the tree.

When they reached the Iei Tree, they plied their axes with skill and toiled vigorously till night came on, but the wood was so hard and so tough they only succeeded in cutting a little below the bark that day. They consoled themselves, however, by reflecting that so far there had appeared no signs of anger from the unknown god forasmuch as no misfortunes had befallen them; so they retired to rest, sanguine that by perseverance their gigantic task would in time be accomplished.

Next morning they returned early to their work, but, to their consternation, they saw that the incisions made by them the day before at the cost of so much labour were obliterated, leaving the trunk of the tree as solid and unscathed as before. Many of the wood-cutters were so superstitious that they feared to approach the tree again, for they were now confirmed in their fear that the place was enchanted; but when their more stoical comrades reminded them of the great peril in which mankind stood, they plucked up courage, and for another day they toiled laboriously, only to find their work obliterated next morning.

As no personal harm had befallen any of them, the wood-cutters determined to continue their attack, but no matter how patiently they worked during the day, the tree would be healed up in the night. They grew more and more mystified and discouraged, and the strain of living in that weird region was becoming intolerable. At last they decided to return to their fellow-men, preferring to endure the foreseen doom of the shadowed world rather than face the unknown and mysterious terrors of the land of the Iei Tree.

As they sat, gloomy and disconsolate, brooding on their defeat, a little grey bird—Ka Phreit, the Khasi wren—came, chirruping and twittering, close to the wood-cutters, and she began to talk to them, urging them to keep up their courage, as she had come to help them. Now, in spite of their spiritless condition, the woodsmen could not help laughing to hear Ka Phreit—the smallest of all the birds—so impudently offering to help them—the picked wood-cutters of the world—to cut down a tree. But when the wren saw them laughing, she chirruped and twittered still louder, and drew still nearer, and with great excitement she said, " No doubt you are great and wise, for you have been chosen for a great task. You are unable to perform it, yet when I come to offer assistance, you laugh at me. It is true that I am the smallest of all the birds, but that has not hindered me from learning the secrets of this forest, which you must also learn before you can cut down the Iei Tree."

On hearing the sage words of the wren, the woodmen felt ashamed for having laughed at her, seeing that she meant nothing but goodwill towards them; so they got up and saluted her, and begged her pardon, and asked her to teach them the secret of the forest. Thus mollified, Ka Phreit informed them that the tree was not healed by any supernatural agency as they had supposed, but that it was U Khla, the big tiger, who came every night to lick the tree and to heal it, for he did not want it to be cut down, as its shadow made it possible for him to prowl for prey in safety.

This news cheered the wood-cutters' hearts and they lost no time in beginning another attack on the Iei Tree, and when night fell, instead of carrying their axes home as before, they planted them in the tree edge outward.

When the tiger came to lick the tree that night (all unconscious that the wren had disclosed the secret to the men), the sharp blades cut his tongue, and he fled in terror, bleeding and howling, and never more returned to hinder the work of the wood-cutters, who, now that they were able to carry on their task undisturbed, succeeded in time in cutting down the Iei Tree.

Thus Ka Phreit, the smallest of all the birds, helped mankind to bring back sunshine and prosperity to the world.

IX

HUNTING THE STAG LAPALANG

ONCE upon a time there lived with its dam on the Plains of Sylhet a young deer whose fame has come down through the ages in Khasi folk-lore. The story of the Stag Lapalang, as he was called, continues to fascinate generation after generation of Khasi youths, and the merry cowboys, as they sit in groups on the wild hill-sides watching their flocks, love to relate the oft-told tale and to describe what they consider the most famous hunt in history.

The Stag Lapalang was the noblest young animal of his race that had ever been seen in the forest and was the pride of his mother's heart. She watched over him with a love not surpassed by the love of a human mother, keeping him jealously at her side, guarding him from all harm.

As he grew older the young stag, conscious of his own matchless grace and splendid strength, began to feel dissatisfied with the narrow confines and limited scope of the forest where they lived and to weary of his mother's constant warnings and counsels. He longed to explore the world and to put his mettle to the test.

His mother had been very indulgent to him all his life and had allowed him to have much of his own way, so there was no restraining him when he expressed his determination to go up to the Khasi Hills to seek begonia leaves to eat. His mother entreated and warned him, but all in vain. He insisted on going, and she watched him sorrowfully as with stately strides and lifted head he went away from his forest home.

Matters went well with the Stag Lapalang at first; he found on the hills plenty of begonia leaves and delicious grass to eat, and he revelled in the freedom of the cool heights. But one day he was seen by some village boys, who immediately gave the alarm, and men soon hurried to the chase: the hunting-cry rang from village to village and echoed from crag to crag. The hunting instincts of the Khasis were roused and men poured forth from every village and hamlet. Oxen were forgotten at the plough; loads were thrown down and scattered; nothing mattered for the moment but the wild exciting chase over hill and valley. Louder sounded the hunting cry, farther it echoed from crag to crag, still wilder grew the chase. From hill to hill and from glen to glen came the hunters, with arrows and spears and staves and swords, hot in pursuit of the Stag Lapalang. He was swift, he was young, he was strong—for days he eluded his pursuers and kept them at bay; but he was only one unarmed creature against a thousand armed men. His fall was inevitable, and one day on the slopes of the Shillong mountain he was surrounded, and after a brave and desperate struggle for his life, the noble young animal died with a thousand arrows quivering in his body.

The lonely mother on the Plains of Sylhet became uneasy at the delay of the return of the Stag Lapalang, and when she heard the echoes of the hunting-cry from the hills her anxiety became more than she could endure. Full of dread misgivings, she set out in quest of her wanderer, but when she reached the Khasi hills, she was told that he had been hunted to death on the slopes of Shillong, and the news broke her heart.

Staggering under the weight of her sorrow, she traversed the rugged paths through the wildwoods, seeking her dead offspring, and as she went her loud heartrending cries were heard throughout the country, arresting every ear. Women, sitting on their hearths, heard it and swooned from the pain of it, and the children hid their faces in dismay; men at work in the fields heard it and bowed their heads and writhed with the anguish of it. Not a shout was raised for a signal at sight of that stricken mother, not a hand was lifted to molest her, and when the huntsmen on the slopes of Shillong heard that bitter cry their shouts of triumph froze upon their lips, and they broke their arrows in shivers.

Never before was heard a lamentation so mournful, so plaintive, so full of sorrow and anguish and misery, as the lament of the mother of the Stag Lapalang as she sought him in death on the slopes of Shillong. The Ancient Khasis were so impressed by this demonstration of deep love and devotion that they felt their own manner of mourning for their dead to be very inferior and orderless, and without meaning. Henceforth they resolved that they also would mourn their departed ones in this devotional way, and many of the formulas used in Khasi lamentations in the present day are those attributed to the mother of the Stag Lapalang when she found him hunted to death on the slopes of Shillong hundreds and hundreds of years ago.

X

THE GODDESSES KA NGOT AND KA IAM

(A Legend of Shillong Peak)

Ka Iam and Ka Ngot, the twin daughters of the god of Shillong, were two very beautiful beings; they were lively and frolicsome, and were indulged and given much freedom by the family. Like all twins they were never happy if long separated. One day the two climbed to the top of the Shillong mountain to survey the country. In the distance they saw the woody plains of Sylhet, and they playfully challenged one another to run a race to see who would reach the plains first.

Ka Ngot was more retiring and timid than her sister, and was half afraid to begin the race; Ka Iam, on the other hand, was venturesome and fearless, and had been called Ka Iam because of her noisy and turbulent disposition. Before the race she spoke very confidently of her own victory, and teased her sister on account of her timidity.

After a little preparation for the journey the twins transformed themselves into two rivers and started to run their race. Ka Ngot, searching for smooth and easy places, meandered slowly, taking long circuits, and came in time to Sylhet; but not finding her sister there, she went forward to Chhatak, and on slowly towards Dewara. Seeing no sign yet of her sister, she became very anxious and turned back to seek her ; and, in turning, she took a long curve which looked in the brilliant sunshine like a curved silver chain, and the Khasis living on the hill-tops, when they saw it, exclaimed with wonder : " Rupatylli, Rupatylli ! " (A silver necklace, a silver necklace !) and to this day that part of the river is known as " Rupatylli."

Ka Iam, full of vigour and ambition, did not linger to look for easy passages, but with a noisy rush she plunged straight in the direction of Shella, the shortest cut she could find. She soon found, however, that the road she had chosen was far more difficult to travel than she had anticipated. Large rocks impeded her path at many points, and she was obliged to spend much time in boring her way through ; but she pitted her young strength against all obstacles, and in time she reached Shella and came in view of the plains, where, to her chagrin, she saw that her sister had reached the goal before her, and was coming back leisurely to meet her. It was a great humiliation, for she had boasted of her victory before the race began, but, hoping to conceal her defeat from the world, she divided herself into five streams, and in that way entered the plains, and joined her sister. The rivers are called after the two goddesses to this day, and are known as " Ka Um Ngot " and " Ka Um Iam " (the river Ngot and the river Iam).

Ever since Ka Ngot won the great race she has been recognised as the greater of the two twins, and more reverence has been paid to her as a goddess. Even in the present day there are many Khasis and Syntengs who will not venture to cross the "Um Ngot" without first sacrificing to the goddess; and when, on their journeys, they happen to catch a glimpse of its waters, they salute and give a greeting of "Khublei" to the goddess Ka Ngot who won the great race.

XI

U BISKUROM

In the beginning of time mankind were very ignorant and did their work with great trouble and labour, for they had no tools and did not understand the way to make them. The Great God saw their difficulty from heaven, and He sent one of the heavenly beings down to the earth, in the likeness of a young man, to teach them. The name of this young man was U Biskurom. He was very noble to look at, and none of the sons of mankind could compare with him; he was also very gentle and good.

He taught mankind many useful crafts. From him they learned to know the value of metals and the way to smelt iron and to make tools, but mankind were very slow to learn, and liked better to muddle in their own old way than to follow the directions given them by U Biskurom, so he had to stay such a long time on the earth that he forgot the way back to heaven. He was, however, so patient and painstaking that at last they learned to make good tools and to use them.

Seeing that U Biskurom excelled them in finishing his instruments, and that he could do double their work in a day, mankind took advantage of his gentleness. They used him to save trouble to themselves, and often demanded work from him that it was impossible for him to do, and when he failed to satisfy them they grew angry and abusive.

One day they made a clay image and called upon U Biskurom to make it alive; when he told them that he had not learnt how to produce life, they abused him and threatened to imprison him until he complied with their request. When U Biskurom saw that they would not listen to reason, he told them that if they wanted him to impart life to their images they must let him go back to heaven to gain the necessary knowledge. Upon this mankind took counsel together what to do. Some feared that if they let him go away he would never return. Others (the majority, however) thought that as the knowledge of how to impart life would be so valuable, it was worth risking a good deal to obtain it; so mankind decided to release U Biskurom.

As he had forgotten the road along which he came to the earth, it was necessary for U Biskurom to invent some means whereby he could go up to heaven; so he told mankind to twine a long piece of string and to make a strong kite on which he could ascend to the sky. So mankind twined a long string and made a strong kite, and U Biskurom rode upon it to the sky. When they said, "Perhaps if we let you go you will not come back," he told them not to let go of the string, so that if he was not allowed to come back, he could write the knowledge on the kite and send it down to them. This satisfied them and they let him go.

When U Biskurom reached heaven the Great God told him that he could not go back to the earth because He had seen how mankind had ill-treated him, and because of their ingratitude and their unholy ambition to impart life. So U Biskurom wrote upon the kite and sent it down to the earth.

When mankind saw the kite descending a great throng came together to read the directions for imparting life, but to their chagrin there was not one among them able to decipher the writing. They consulted together what to do, for they were very angry with U Biskurom, and they decided to send a great shout to heaven, which would cause such a volley that the concussion would kill U Biskurom.

U Biskurom laughed when he saw their folly, and in order to make them still more foolish, he caused some drops of blood to fall down from heaven, and when mankind saw these drops of blood they concluded that he had been killed by the force of their great shout.

Because of their ingratitude and their uplifted pride mankind have remained in great ignorance, and all the knowledge they possess is very imperfect and gained at great labour and expense.

XII

U THLEN, THE SNAKE-VAMPIRE

U THLEN is one of the legendary Khasi gods, whose worship is limited to a few clans and families. From participation in it all right-thinking Khasis recoil with loathing and horror, inasmuch as it involves the perpetration of crimes, for this god can only be propitiated by offerings of human sacrifices, with many revolting and barbaric rites.

The clans who are reputed to be the devotees and worshippers of the Thlen are regarded with aversion and fear throughout the country, and to them are attributed many kinds of atrocities, such as the kidnapping of children, murders and attempted murders, and many are the tales of hair-breadth escapes from the clutches of these miscreants, who are known as *Nongshohnohs*. Within quite recent times murders have been committed which are still shrouded in mystery, but which are said to have indications that the victims were killed for the purpose of Thlen sacrifice.

The following folk-tale purports to give an account of the origin and propagation of U Thlen, the most remorseless and cruel of all the Khasi deities.

According to tradition the Hima (state) of Cherra was, in olden times, the haunt of many famous *Bleis* (gods) who dominated the lives of men. These deities were said to dwell in certain localities, which in consequence came to be recognised as sacred places, and frequently to be called after the names of the *Bleis*. Foremost among these gods was U Mawlong Siem, and the hill where he was supposed to dwell is called after his name to the present day, and the inhabitants of certain villages still offer sacrifices to him.

In common with mankind, U Mawlong Siem is described as having a family, who, also in common with mankind, took pleasure in dancing and festivity. It is said that people sometimes hear the sound of revelry and the beating of drums within the mountain, supposed to be the drums of U Mawlong Siem beaten to the accompaniment of the dancing of his children, the sound of which invariably portends the death of a Siem or some great personage.

The only one of his family whose name and history have been transmitted was a daughter called Ka Kma Kharai, which signifies one that roams about in trenches or hidden nooks. She was well known in the *Blei*-world, and she possessed the power of assuming whatever form she pleased. She often assumed the form of a woman and mingled with mankind without anybody suspecting her identity. Many of the *Bleis* sought her in marriage, but U Mawlong Siem, her father, would never give his consent, lest his prestige be lowered among the *Bleis*.

There was one suitor whom Ka Kma Kharai specially favoured. He was the god of Umwai, but her father forbade the union so sternly as to dispel all the hopes of the lovers. This so angered the young goddess that henceforth she rebelled openly against her father, and by way of retaliation she encouraged the attentions of strange and undesirable lovers.

When it was discovered that she was with child, she fled from her home, fearing the wrath of her father, and put herself under the protection of her maternal uncle, who lived in the Pomdoloi cave, and was one of the famous dragons, or Yak Jakors of the country.

THE HAUNT OF KA KMA KHARAI.

In this cave a son was born to her, who proved to be a monster of hideous aspect, having the form of a snake and the characteristics of a vampire, who could be appeased only when fed with human blood. This monster they called U Thlen.

Unlike his mother, U Thlen could not transform himself into any likeness but that of a snake, but he had power to diminish or to enlarge his size at will. Sometimes he appeared so small as to be no bigger than a string of fine thread, at other times he expanded himself to such dimensions that he could swallow a man bodily.

In those days there was much intercourse between the *Bleis* and mankind. The latter were privileged to attend the *Iew-blei*—the fair of the *Bleis*—at Lynghingkhongkhen, the way to which passed the Pomdoloi cave, and many unwary and unprotected travellers fell a prey to the greed of U Thlen and his associates.

The commonest mode by which these poor unfortunates were lured to their doom was through the blandishments of Ka Kma Kharai, who approached them in the form of a woman merchant, and dazzled them with the brilliancy of the jewelry she offered for sale. She refrained from killing her captives on occasions, but induced them by promises of riches and immunity to pledge themselves to the services of U Thlen, her son. To such as these she gave a magic ring, known in ancient lore as the Yngkuid Ring (Sati Yngkuid) which was believed to possess magic that enabled the owners of the ring to obtain all the desires of their hearts, but this magic was dormant until the owners fulfilled their obligations to U Thlen and brought him human victims to feed upon.

The method by which U Yak Jakor captured his victims was to waylay lonely travellers and to club them to death. U Thlen himself, when he grew old enough, also hunted men to death, so that between the three murderers the ravages made upon mankind were becoming grievous and intolerable.

Mankind sought divinations and offered sacrifices to the gods for the cessation of these atrocities, upon which a Durbar of the *Bleis* was called. U Mawlong

Siem, who was a powerful *Blei* and a blood-relation of the murderers, overruled the Durbar, declaring that no authority could deprive the *Bleis*, or the demons, of any power they possessed, be it for good or for evil; but to mitigate the distress of mankind a decree was issued, restricting the number of people to be devoured to half the number of captives. If U Thlen captured two victims, one was to be released, if he captured ten, five were to be released. It transpired, however, that this decree helped but little to allay the sufferings of mankind, for murders continued at an appalling rate.

Mankind again sought divination and took counsel together, and it was made evident that the only one who could successfully help them was U Suidnoh (the fleeting demon), an erratic and insignificant being who haunted the forest of Lait-rngew to the north of Cherra. The Khasis hitherto had never recognised him as worthy of homage, but they went to offer him sacrifices then, according to the divinations. U Suidnoh volunteered to rescue them, but affirmed that the Snake could never be overcome without the sanction of a *Blei*, and inasmuch as the *Bleis* of the Cherra *Hima* had already refused their aid, he urged them to go and sacrifice to U 'Lei Shillong—the god of the Shillong mountain—and to invoke his aid and win his favour. So mankind offered sacrifices to U 'Lei Shillong, and received his sanction to wage war against U Thlen.

U Suidnoh, equipped in all his strength, went forth to Pomdoloi and ordered the Khasis to bring to him many fat pigs and goats. These he killed and carried regularly to feed the Thlen in the cave, and this was the manner in which he made his offering. He bored a large hole in a rock roofing the cave, so that the

SACRED GROVE AND MONOLITHS.

carcases might be passed down without being seen by U Thlen, and so he would not discover that they were not human bodies. He assumed the voice and manner of a Thlen worshipper and called out: "My uncle, I have brought my tribute, open your mouth that I may feed you." U Thlen is described as being slothful and sleepy, never rousing himself except to seek food. When he heard the call from above he would shake himself and expand to a great size, and open wide his jaws, into which the meat offering was thrust. In this way mankind had respite for a time, and the hunting of men ceased.

It was evident, however, that they must resort to some other measures, for it was impossible to continue to keep up the supply of fat animals. The Khasis began to grumble at the extravagant proceedings of U Suidnoh, but he always replied to their complaints with the words, "*Koit, koit,*" signifying that all was well. After a time he told them to hire the services of U Ramhah, the giant, to assist him in his final struggle against the vampire. When U Ramhah came he bade him build a smelting-house near the cave, and to make a pair of giant tongs, and such was the strength of U Ramhah that it only took him one day to build the smelting-house and to make the giant tongs. Next day U Suidnoh told him to heat a large piece of iron, and to bring it when it was red-hot in the big tongs to the rock on the top of the cave. When this was done U Suidnoh called out according to his custom: "My uncle, I have brought my tribute, open your mouth that I may feed you"; so the Thlen shook himself and expanded his body to a gigantic size, and opened his jaws for the offering, whereupon the red-hot iron was thrust in. Upon this there followed the most terrible contortions of the Thlen's body, as he tossed about, writhing in his death agony, till the earth shook so violently that U Suidnoh and U Ramhah swooned from the concussion. When the disturbance subsided, and they had revived, they looked into the cave and found U Thlen lying dead.

U Suidnoh sounded a big drum to summon the people together, and great jubilation and dancing took place when it was announced that their enemy was dead. From that time the Khasis have offered sacrifices to U Suidnoh, and he is held in great honour.

The people held a council to consider how to dispose of the body of the Thlen, and it was decided that to make their triumph complete it was better to prepare a feast and to eat the body of U Thlen, so the carcase was dragged out of the cave and was divided on a flat rock into two portions. One portion was given to the people of the plains from the East, to be cooked after their manner, the other was given to the Khasis from the hills and the West to be cooked after their manner. The marks of the axe are said to be seen on the rock to this day, and the place is called *Dain Thlen* (the cutting of the Thlen). The hole which was bored by U Suidnoh in the top of the cave is also said to be visible to this day.

It happened that more people came to the feast from the plains than from the hills; moreover, they were accustomed to eat eels and snakes, so they considered the Thlen meat very palatable and savoury. They ate the whole of their portion and departed to their villages happily, and they were never afterwards troubled by Thlens. On the other hand the Khasis were unused to the flesh of reptiles, and they found the Thlen meat very unsavoury and strange-flavoured, so that when their feasting was done, a great portion of the meat remained uneaten.

This caused no little perplexity, for it was deemed possible for the Thlen to come and reanimate the unconsumed portions of his body, so they kindled a big fire to burn all the fragments of meat to ashes, after which they gave a glad shout, believing themselves for ever safe from the ravages of U Thlen.

A certain woman, whose son had neglected his duties and stayed away from the feast, was sorely troubled in her mind, fearing that some ill luck might befall him, and a curse come on the family, because her son had wilfully disregarded the feast of conquest. While helping to gather the fragments of meat for burning, she surreptitiously hid a piece in the fold of her dress to take home to her son. When she reached her house she put the meat away in a covcred vessel pending her son's arrival. When the son returned he brought news of many misfortunes which he had met that day, and particularly of the loss of much money, which loss he attributed to his neglect of the important feast; but when his mother told him how she had contrived to bring him a little of the Thlen meat, he was somewhat cheered, hoping that by this participation he might be helped to retrieve his fallen fortunes. To their dismay, when they uncovered the vessel, there was no meat left, only a tiny live snake wriggling about. They were preparing to destroy it when the little snake began to speak to them in their own tongue, beseeching them not to kill him. He said he was U Thlen come back to life, and that he was there by the decrees of the

Bleis to bring them good fortune for as long as they gave him harbour and tribute.

It was a great temptation, coming as it did, when they had met with great losses, so, without thinking much of the consequences, they allowed the Thlen to live, harbouring it in secret without the knowledge of outsiders.

When U Thlen had fully regained his vitality, he demanded human sacrifices from them, which made them shudder with horror. But U Thlen was relentless, and threatened to devour them as a family, if they did not comply with his request, and when they saw one member of the family after another beginning to languish, fear for their lives drove them to hunt their fellow-men and to murder them, to propitiate U Thlen and to keep his good favour. Gradually U Thlen cast his sway over other families also, and won them to give him tribute. As his devotees increased he reproduced himself mysteriously, so that in place of one Thlen living in a cave where everybody knew him to be, there arose many Thlens, living concealed in the houses of the *Nongshohnohs* who, to preserve their own safety and the goodwill of U Thlen, have become men-hunters and murderers, of whom the Khasis live in deadly fear to this day.

XIII

HOW THE DOG CAME TO LIVE WITH MAN

In the happy olden days, when the animals lived together at peace in the forest, they used to hold fairs and markets after the manner of mankind. The most important fair of all was called "Ka Iew Luri Lura" (the Fair of Luri Lura), which was held at stated intervals in the Bhoi (forest) country. Thither gathered all the animals, each one bringing some article of merchandise, according to the decree which demanded that every animal that came to the fair should bring something to sell. No matter whether he was young or old, rich or poor, no one was to come empty-handed, for they wanted to enhance the popularity of the market. U Khla, the tiger, was appointed governor of the fair.

Man was excluded from these fairs as he was looked upon as an enemy. He used to hunt the animals with his bow and arrows, so they had ceased to fraternise with him and kept out of his way. But one day the dog left his own kindred in the jungle, and became the attendant of Man. The following story tells how that came to pass.

One day U Ksew, the dog, walked abroad in search of goods to sell at the fair. The other animals were thrifty and industrious, they worked to produce their merchandise, but the dog, being of an indolent nature, did not like to work, though he was very desirous to go to the fair. So, to avoid the censure of his neighbours and the punishment of the governor of the fair, he set out in search of something he could get without much labour to himself. He trudged about the country all day, inquiring at many villages, but when evening-time

AT THE FOOT OF THE SHILLONG MOUNTAINS.

came he had not succeeded in purchasing any suitable goods, and he began to fear that he would have to forgo the pleasure of attending the fair after all.

Just as the sun was setting he found himself on the outskirts of Saddew village, on the slopes of the Shillong Mountain, and as he sniffed the air he became aware of a strong and peculiar odour, which he guessed came from some cooked food. Being hungry after his long tramp, he pushed his way forward, following the scent till he came to a house right in the middle of the village,where he saw the family at dinner, which he noticed they were eating with evident relish. The dinner consisted of fermented Khasi beans, known as *ktung rymbai*, from which the strong smell emanated.

The Khasis are naturally a very cordial and hospitable people, and when the good wife of the house saw the dog standing outside looking wistfully at them she invited him to partake of what food there was left in the pot. U Ksew thankfully accepted, and by reason of his great hunger he ate heartily, regardless of the strange flavour and smell of the food, and he considered the *ktung rymbai* very palatable.

It dawned on him that here, quite by accident, he had found a novel and marketable produce to take to the fair; and it happened that the kindly family who had entertained him had a quantity of the stuff for sale which they kept in earthen jars, sealed with clay to retain ite flavour. After a little palaver according to custom, a bargain was struck, and U Ksew became the owner of one good-sized jar of *ktung rymbai*, which he cheerfully took on his back. He made his way across the hills to Luri Lura fair, chuckling to himself as he anticipated the sensation he would create and the profits he would gain, and the praise he would win for being so enterprising.

On the way he encountered many of the animals who like himself were all going to Luri Lura, and carrying merchandise on their backs to sell at the fair: to them U Ksew boasted of the wonderful food he had discovered and was bringing with him to the market in the earthen jar under the clay seal. He talked so much about it that the contents of the earthen jar became the general topic of conversation between the animals, for never had such an article been known at Luri Lura.

When he arrived at the fair the dog walked in with great consequence, and installed himself and his earthen jar in the most central place with much clatter and ostentation. Then he began to shout at the top of his voice, "Come and buy my good food," and what with his boastings on the road and the noise he made at the fair, a very large company gathered round him, stretching their necks to have a glimpse at the strange-looking jar, and burning with curiosity to see the much-advertised contents.

U Ksew, with great importance, proceeded to uncover the jar; but as soon as he broke the clay seal a puff of the most unsavoury and fœtid odour issued forth and drove all the animals scrambling to a safe distance, much to the dog's discomfiture and the merriment of the crowd. They hooted and jeered, and made all sorts of disparaging remarks till U Ksew felt himself covered with shame.

The stag pushed forward, and to show his disdain he contemptuously kicked the earthen jar till it broke. This increased the laughter and the jeering, and more of the animals came forward, and they began to trample the *ktung rymbai* in the mud, taking no notice of the protestations of U Ksew, who felt himself very unjustly treated. He went to U Khla, the governor of the fair, to ask for redress, but here again he was met with ridicule and scorn, and told that he deserved all the treatment he had received for filling the market-place with such a stench.

At last U Ksew's patience wore out, he grew snappish and angry, and with loud barks and snarls he began to curse the animals with many curses, threatening to be avenged upon them all some day. At the time no one heeded his curses and threats, for the dog was but a contemptible animal in their estimation, and it was not thought possible for him to work much harm. Yet even on that day a part of his curse came true, for the animals found to their dismay that the smell of the *ktung rymbai* clung to their paws and their hoofs, and could not be obliterated; so the laughter was not all on their side.

Humiliated and angry, the dog determined to leave the fair and the forest and his own tribe, and to seek more congenial surroundings; so he went away from Luri Lura, never to return, and came once more to Saddew village, to the house of the family from whom he had bought the offending food. When the master of the house heard the story of the ill-treatment he had suffered from the animals, he pitied U Ksew, and he also considered that the insults touched himself as well as the dog, inasmuch as it was he who had prepared and sold the *ktung rymbai*. So he spoke consolingly to U Ksew and patted his head and told him to remain in the village with him, and that he would protect him and help him to avenge his wrongs upon the animals.

After the coming of the dog, Man became a very successful hunter, for the dog, who always accompanied him when he went out to hunt, was able to follow the trail of the animals by the smell of the *ktung rymbai*, which adhered to their feet. Thus the animals lived to rue the day when they played their foolish pranks on U Ksew and his earthen jar at the fair of Luri Lura.

Man, having other occupations, could not always go abroad to the jungle to hunt; so in order to secure a supply of meat for himself during the non-hunting seasons he tamed pigs and kept them at hand in the village. When the dog came he shared the dwelling and the meals of the pig, U Sniang; they spent their days in idleness, living on the bounty of Man.

One evening, as Man was returning from his field, tired with the day's toil, he noticed the two idle animals and he said to himself—"It is very foolish of me to do all the hard work myself while these two well-fed creatures are lying idle. They ought to take a turn at doing some work for their food."

The following morning Man commanded the two animals to go to the field to plough in his stead. When they arrived there U Sniang, in obedience to his master's orders, began to dig with his snout, and by nightfall had managed to furrow quite a large patch of the field; but U Ksew, according to his indolent habits, did no work at all. He lay in the shade all day, or amused himself by snapping at the flies. In the evening, when it was time to go home, he would start running backwards and forwards over the furrows, much to the annoyance of the pig.

The same thing happened for many days in succession, till the patience of the pig was exhausted, and on their return from the field one evening he went and informed their master of the conduct of the dog, how he was idling the whole day and leaving all the work for him to do.

The master was loth to believe these charges against U Ksew, whom he had found such an active and willing helper in the chase: he therefore determined to go and examine the field. When he came there he found only a few of the footprints of the pig, while those of the dog were all over the furrows. He at once concluded that U Sniang had falsely charged his friend, and he was exceedingly wroth with him.

When he came home, Man called the two animals to him, and he spoke very angrily to U Sniang, and told him that henceforth he would have to live in a little sty by himself, and to eat only the refuse from Man's table and other common food, as a punishment for making false charges against his friend; but the dog would be privileged to live in the house with his master, and to share the food of his master's family.

Thus it was that the dog came to live with Man.

XIV

THE ORIGIN OF BETEL AND TOBACCO

LONG, long ago two boys lived in a village on the slopes of the hills, who were very fond of one another and were inseparable companions. The name of one was U Riwbha ; he was the son of one of the wealthiest men in the country. The other was called U Baduk, who belonged to one of the lowly families ; but the difference in station was no barrier to the affection of the children for one another. Every day they sought one another out, and together they roamed abroad in the fields and the forests, learning to know the birds and the flowers ; together they learned to swim in the rivers, together they learned to use the bow and arrow, and to play on the flute. They loved the same pastimes and knew the same friends.

As they grew up they were not able to spend so much time together. U Riwbha had to overlook his father's property, which involved many days' absence from the village ; while U Baduk went every day to labour in the fields to earn his own rice and to help his parents, who were poor. But the old friendship remained as firm as ever between the two young men, they trusted one another fully, and the one kept no secrets from the other.

In the course of time they took to themselves wives and became the heads of families. U Riwbha's wife, like himself, belonged to one of the wealthy families, so that by his marriage his influence in the village increased, and he became very rich and prosperous. U Baduk also married into his own class and went to live in a distant

A VIEW IN THE REPUTED REGION WHERE U RAMHAH THE GIANT COMMITTED HIS ATROCITIES.

village, but he never gathered riches like his friend; nevertheless he was very happy. He had a good and thrifty wife, and side by side they daily toiled in the fields to supply their simple wants as a family.

Thus circumstances kept the two friends apart, for they seldom met. The old regard was not in the least abated by absence, rather the bond seemed to be drawn closer and closer as the years went by. Occasionally U Baduk journeyed to his native village to see his people and friends, and on these occasions nowhere was he made more welcome than in the house of his friend U Riwbha, who insisted upon his spending the greater part of his time with him, and partaking of many sumptuous meals at his house. Thus the two old comrades renewed their intimacy and affection.

On his return home from one such visit U Baduk's wife told him that their neighbours had been talking a great deal and making disparaging remarks about the intimacy between them and their wealthy friend, hinting that no such friendship existed, that it was only U Baduk's boast that he had rich friends in his own village. If there were such an intimacy as he pretended, why had his rich friend never come to see them when U Baduk was constantly going to visit him? He was vexed to hear this, not so much because they condemned him, but because they were casting aspersions on his best friend, so he determined to invite his friend to pay them a visit.

When U Baduk paid his next visit to his village, and had as usual accepted the hospitality of his friend, he ventured to say, "I am always coming to see you and partaking of your hospitality, but you have not been to see me once since I got married."

To this U Riwbha replied, "Very true, my dear friend, very true, but do not take it amiss that I never thought of this before. You know that I have much business on my hands, and have no leisure like many people to take my pleasures; but I have been too remiss towards you, and I must make haste to remedy my fault. Give my greeting to your wife, and tell her that I will start from here to-morrow to come to pay you both a visit, and to give myself the pleasure of tasting a dish of her curry and rice."

Highly gratified and pleased, U Baduk hastened home to tell his wife of his friend's projected visit, and urged her to rouse herself and to cook the most savoury meal she was capable of. She too was very pleased to hear that the man they respected and loved so much was coming to see them; but she said, "It has come very suddenly, when I am not prepared; we have neither fish nor rice in the house."

"That is indeed unfortunate," said the husband, "but we have kind neighbours from whom we have never asked a favour before. You must go out and borrow what is wanted from them, for it would be too great a disgrace not to have food to place before our friend when he comes."

The wife went out as requested by her husband, but although she walked the whole length of the village there was no one who could spare her any rice or fish, and she returned home gloomy and disheartened and told her husband of her ill-success. When U Baduk heard this bad news he was extremely troubled and said, "What sort of a world is this to live in, where a morsel of food cannot be obtained to offer hospitality to a friend? It is better to die than to live." Whereupon he seized a knife and stabbed himself to death.

When the wife saw that her good husband was dead, she was smitten with inconsolable grief, and she cried out, "What is there for me to live for now? It is better that I also should die." Thereupon she in her turn seized the knife and stabbed herself to death.

It happened that a notorious robber called U Nongtuh was wandering through the village that night, and, as it was cold, he bethought himself of sneaking into one of the houses where the family had gone to sleep, to warm himself. He saw that a fire was burning in U Baduk's house, and that it was very silent within. He determined to enter. "They are hard-working people," said he to himself, "and will sleep soundly; I can safely sit and warm myself without their knowing anything about me." So he squatted down comfortably on the hearth, not knowing that the two dead bodies lay on the floor close to him.

Before long the warmth made him drowsy, and without thinking U Nongtuh fell asleep, and did not awake until the day was dawning; he jumped up hastily, hoping to escape before the village was astir, but he saw the two dead bodies and was greatly terrified. A great trembling took him, and he began to mutter wildly, "What an unfortunate man I am to have entered this house! The neighbours will say that I killed these people; it will be useless for me to deny it, for I have such an evil reputation nobody will believe me. It is better for me to die by my own hand here than to be caught by the villagers, and be put to death like a murderer." Whereupon he seized the knife and stabbed himself to death; so there were three victims on the floor, lying dead side by side, all because there was no food in the house to offer hospitality to a friend.

The morning advanced, and when the neighbours noticed that no one stirred abroad from U Baduk's house they flocked there to find out what was the matter. When they saw the three dead bodies they were filled with sadness and compunction, for they remembered how they had refused to lend them food the night before, to prepare entertainment for their friend.

In the course of the day U Riwbha arrived according to the promise made to his friend, and when he was told of the terrible tragedy his sorrow knew no bounds; he sat wailing and mourning by the body of the friend that he loved best, and would not be comforted. "Alas!" he wailed, "that a man should lose such a true friend because the world is become so hard for the poor that to entertain a friend is a greater burden than they can bear."

For many hours he wept and sorrowed, praying to the Great God to show a way of keeping up the customs of hospitality without the poor having to suffer and be crushed, as his own good friend had been crushed.

Just about that time the Great God walked abroad to look on the universe, and he saw the sorrow of U Riwbha, and took pity on his tears, and made known that from henceforth He would cause to grow three valuable plants, which were to be used by mankind in future as the means of entertainment, whereby the poor as well as the rich could indulge in the entertainment of friends without being burdened. Immediately three trees which had never been known to mankind before were seen springing up from the ground where the dead bodies lay. They were the Betel, the Pan, and the Tobacco.

From that time it became a point of etiquette in Khasi households, rich and poor alike, to offer betel nut and pan or a whiff of tobacco from the hookah to friends when they make calls.

XV

THE STAG AND THE SNAIL

On the day of the animals' fair at Luri Lura, the stag and the snail met. It was a very hot day, and the animals as they travelled to the fair eagerly sought the shelter of the trees. There was a large Rubber grove in the forest, and thither many of the animals hasted, panting from the great heat, and there laid down their burdens for a while and rested in the cool shades.

It was a familiar rendezvous, and many of the animals turned there, as much from habit as from fatigue, glad to meet old acquaintances. On the day which concerns this story there was an unusually large throng, and they chatted together sociably about the different events of their lives and the circumstances of their neighbours.

In one corner a group were noisily comparing notes with one another about the length of time it had taken them to travel certain distances. In this group was the stag, who monopolised the conversation, and boasted of his own speed, and the buffalo, trying to be affable, said that they were bound to admit that the stag was now the swiftest animal in the jungle, since the dog had run away to Man, and the entire company nodded in agreement.

There was, however, a little grey snail in the grass with her shell on her back, who was very disgusted with the boastings of the animals, especially of the stag, as if swiftness was the only virtue to which an animal ought to aspire. In order to put a stop to their talk, she called out mockingly for them to look at the lather that covered their bodies from over-exertion, and to compare her own cool skin, which had not perspired at all in spite of the journey; consequently, she claimed the honours for good travelling for herself.

This was received with much displeasure by the animals, who felt that their dignity had been flouted, for the snail was an insect in their estimation, not fit to be admitted to their august company. The stag began to canter gracefully round the grove to prove his superiority, his fellow animals applauding admiringly; but the little snail was not to be silenced, and to show her contempt she challenged the stag to run a long race with her, declaring that she would beat him.

Many of the animals urged the stag not to heed the challenge of the snail, as it was only given to affront him, but he said that unless he would run she would always insult him and call him a coward who had shown fear of a snail. So it was settled that the stag and the snail should run a long race, from the Rubber grove to the top of Mount Shillong, on the animals' return from Luri Lura.

The name of this little grey snail was Ka Mattah. As soon as the animals left the grove she summoned together all her tribe to consider how to proceed so as to beat the stag in the long race. Many of the snail family found fault with her for her foolish challenge, but they were all prepared to help her out of her difficulty, and to save her from the disgrace of defeat. It was decided in the family council that the snails should form themselves into a long line edging the path all the way from the Rubber grove to Mount Shillong, and hide themselves in the grass, so as not to be discovered by the stag. So the snails dispersed and formed themselves into a long line on the edge of the path.

As soon as they had sold their wares, the animals hastened to the grove, laughing among themselves as they walked at the foolishness of Ka Mattah in setting herself up against the swiftest of the animals, and they planned how to make her the general laughing-stock of the jungle for her audacity. When they reached the Rubber grove they found Ka Mattah ready for the race, having discarded her cumbersome shell and put herself into a racing attitude on the path, which caused them no little amusement. As soon as the signal was given she dived into the grass and was lost to sight, while the stag cantered towards the mountains. After going some distance, he stopped, thinking that there would be no need to run further, as he imagined that the snail was far behind and likely to have given up the race; so he called out, "Heigh, Mattah, art thou coming?"

To his surprise, the voice of the snail answered close beside him saying, "I am here, I am here." Thereupon he ran on more swiftly, but after running several miles he stopped again and called out as before, "Heigh, Mattah, art thou coming?" And again the voice answered close to his heels, "I am here, I am here"; upon which the stag tore off at a terrific pace through the forest, only stopping at intervals to call out to the snail. As often as he called, the voice answered close to his feet, "I am here, I am here," which set him racing with ever-increasing speed. When he reached the Iei Tree Mountain, he was panting and quivering from his great exertions and longed to lie down to rest, but he saw before him the goal to which he was bound, and spurred himself to a last effort. He was so exhausted as he climbed up the slopes of Shillong that he was giddy and faint, and could scarcely move his wearied limbs, and, to his dismay, before he reached the summit, he heard the tormenting voice of the snail calling out from the goal, "I have won, I have won."

Exhausted and defeated, the stag threw himself full length on the ground, and his disappointment and the sickness due to the terrible strain he had put on himself caused him to spit out his gall-bladder. To this day no gall-bladder is to be found in the anatomy of the stag; so he carries in his body the token of the great defeat he sustained through the wiles of Ka Mattah, the little grey snail, and the pathetic look has never gone out of his eyes.

XVI

THE LEAP OF KA LIKAI

"The Leap of Ka Likai" is the name given to a beautiful waterfall on the Khasi Hills, a few miles to the west of Cherrapoonjee, which, at certain points, is visible from great distances, while the roar and the echoes of its waters are to be heard for miles. The view is one of exceptional beauty, and many visitors are attracted to see it. The clear chattering stream is seen emerging from its wild mountain home, dashing over the high precipice into the shadows of a deep gorge, flinging upwards, as it falls, clouds of tremulous spray, which wreathe and coil around majestic rocks, creating countless small rainbows which dance and quiver in a maze of palms and ferns and blossoming shrubs.

The place is so remote and so still, as if every sound had been awed into a hush, except the thunderous boom of the torrent with its distant echoes moaning and shrieking like a spirit in anguish, that the whole locality seems weird and uncanny, suggestive of terrible possibilities. This, probably, accounts for the gruesome tradition amongst the Khasis which has been associated with this waterfall from time immemorial. It runs as follows:

Once upon a time there lived a young married woman

THE LEAP OF KA LIKAI.

called Ka Likai, in the village of Rangjirteh, on the hill above the Falls. She and her husband lived very happily together and rejoiced in the possession of a baby girl of great beauty. The young husband died when the child was still a babe, and from that time Ka Likai's whole heart became wrapped up in the child.

She found it very hard to earn enough money to maintain them both, so she was persuaded to marry again, thinking to have her own burden lightened, and to obtain more comforts for her child.

The new husband was a selfish and a somewhat brutal man; he was exceedingly jealous of his little step-daughter, because his wife paid her so much attention, and when he found that he had been accepted as a husband by Ka Likai merely for the benefit of the child, he was so mortified that he grew to hate her and determined to do her some mischief.

He became sulky in the home and refused to go out to work, but he forced his wife to go every day, and during her absence he bullied and ill-treated the child. One day Ka Likai had to go on a long journey to carry iron ore, and this gave the cruel stepfather the opportunity he sought to carry out his evil purpose, and he killed the child. So depraved had he become and so demoniacal was his hatred, that he determined to inflict even a worse horror upon his wife; he took portions of the body and cooked them against the mother's return, and waited in silence for her coming.

When Ka Likai reached her home in the evening, she was surprised to find her husband in a seemingly kinder mood than he had shown for a long time, having cooked her supper and set it ready for her, with unusual consideration. She noticed the absence of the child, and immediately asked where she was, but the man's plausible answer that she had just gone out to play dispelled every misgiving, and she sat down to eat without a suspicion of evil.

After finishing her supper, she drew forward the betel-nut basket to prepare betel and pan to chew, according to custom after a meal. It happened that one of the hands of the murdered girl had been left by the stepfather in this basket, and the mother at once saw and recognised it. She wildly demanded the meaning of the awful discovery, whereupon the man confessed his crime, and also told her how she herself had eaten of the flesh of her own child.

The terrible and overwhelming revelation took away the mother's reason. She rose distractedly, and, running to the edge of the precipice, threw herself into the abyss. Ever since then the Falls have been called "The Leap of Ka Likai," and the doleful moans of their echoes are said to be the echoes of Ka Likai's anguished cries.

To this day, when widows with children are contemplating second marriages, they are cautioned to be careful and to use judgement, with the warning, "Remember Ka Likai."

XVII

WHAT CAUSED THE SHADOWS ON THE MOON

In the early ages there lived a family of deities, consisting of a mother and four children—three daughters and one son. They lived very happily for many long years, the children showing great respect to their mother and to one another. Their names were Ka Um (Water), Ka Ding (Fire), and Ka Sngi (the Sun), and the boy was called U Bnai (the Moon). They were all very noble and beautiful to look upon, as became their high destiny, but it was universally agreed that Ka Sngi and U Bnai, the two youngest, possessed greater beauty and loveliness than the two elder sisters. In those days the moon was equal to the sun in brightness and splendour.

When U Bnai grew up he began to show somewhat wayward tendencies ; he came and went at his own will, without consulting his mother or his sisters, and consorted with companions far beneath him in rank. Sometimes he would absent himself from home for many days, and none of his family knew whither he wandered. His mother often remonstrated with him, as is right for every mother to do, and she and his sisters endeavoured to guide him into more decorous habits, but he was wilful and self-indulgent, thinking that he had a right to more liberty than his women-folk allowed him. By degrees he abandoned himself to a life of pleasure and wild pursuits, paying no heed to the advice and warnings of his elders.

Once he followed some of his low associates into the nether regions and spent a long time in that land of goblins and vice. After a while his thoughts came back to his family and his erstwhile radiant home, and a longing to see them came over him, so he quitted the nether regions, and left his evil companions, and returned to his home and his kindred.

He had gazed so long on the hideous faces of the inhabitants of the dark world, that he was dazzled by the beauty of his sister Ka Sngi, who came to meet him with smiles and joy for his return. He had also lost the right perception of duty and honour, and, instead of greeting her as his sister, he went to his mother and with unbrotherly wantonness demanded the hand of Ka Sngi in marriage, saying that he had travelled throughout many worlds, and had seen the sons of all nations, but there was no suitor to be found in the whole universe whose beauty could match that of Ka Sngi, except himself. Consequently he said that it behoved his mother to give countenance to his suit and to arrange the marriage.

This caused the mother much grief, and she dismissed her son from her presence in dishonour. Ka Sngi, when she heard of his design, was enraged because of his unchaste proposal, and in anger she went forth to seek her brother. When she found him she forgot her usual dignity and decorum, and, lifting a handful of hot ashes, she threw it into U Bnai's face. The ashes scorched his flesh so deeply that the marks have remained on his face to this day. Ever since then the light of the moon has been pale, marred by dark shadows, and that is the reason he does not show his face in the day-time.

XVIII

U KSUID TYNJANG

THE Ancient Khasis were wont to people all their beautiful hills and forests with innumerable supernatural beings, who were supposed to be working in the world either for good or for evil, and dominating all the events of men's lives. There were *Bleis* (gods) of all grades, and *Ksuids* (demons or goblins) without number, and *Puris* (sprites or fairies), visible and invisible, to be encountered everywhere. The religious observances of the Khasis are mainly intended to fulfil obligations supposed to be imposed upon them by these imaginary beings, who are described as quick to take offence and difficult to appease; hence the many and complicated ceremonies which the Khasi religion demands.

One of the most familiar names in ancient lore is that of U Ksuid Tynjang, a deformed and lame demon who haunted the forests and tormented mankind, and for his misdeeds had been doomed to suffer from an incurable and loathsome itching disease, which could only be allayed by the touch of a human hand. All the stories related of this repulsive demon are concerned with his forbidding personality and the tortures he inflicted on the victims he captured purposely to force them to rub his body and relieve the terrible itching to which he had been doomed. He used to tickle them to death with his deformed and claw-like hands if they tried to desist from their sickening task.

To lure people into his grasp, he used to imitate the human voice and to shout "*Kaw-hoit, Kaw-hoit!*" the common signal-cry of people who lose their companions or their way—a cry to which all humane travellers

THE REPUTED HAUNT OF U KSUID TYNJANG.

quickly respond, for it is considered equivalent to murder to ignore the signal-cry without going to the rescue. In this way U Ksuid Tynjang was able to locate the whereabouts of lonely wanderers, and thither he would direct his unsteady steps, skipping and hobbling through the jungle, until he came up to them and made them his captives.

In those days a great fair was periodically held at the foot of the Hills, and to this the Khasis from all over the country were wont to resort, especially the younger folk, who were fond of pleasure and liked to see the show of fine cloths brought there for sale. It happened that two young sisters from the Hills, Ka Thei and Ka Duh, with their brother, attended one of these fairs in the company of some of their neighbours. It was their first visit to a fair, and they were so taken up with the wonders of it that they forgot all about the time, and walked to and fro, gazing at the strange people and wares, until unconsciously they drifted away from their friends. It was now growing late, and Ka Thei, the eldest sister, anxiously bade the others cling to her that they might retrace their steps and if possible find their companions; but although they walked from one end of the fair to the other, they met nobody they knew. By this they were in great dismay, and they determined to start for home as fast as they could, hoping to overtake their friends on the way. Evidently every one was far ahead, for though they walked very fast and called out at intervals, they saw no signs of a friend and heard no response, and by the time they reached the Shillong forests, when they were yet some miles from home, night closed upon them, and they lost their way in the dense dark jungle. It was hopeless to try and proceed further, for the path could not be traced in the darkness, so the three timid young travellers sat down, footsore and forlorn, crushed down with foreboding and fear.

Just then they heard a loud cry in the distance, *Kaw-hoit!* and they all thought it was the cry of one of their friends signalling to them, and the three shouted back in chorus *Kaw-hoit!* and waited expectantly for some one to appear. To their horror they saw approaching, not a friend as they had expected, but the deformed and diseased figure of a hideous *Ksuid*, upon which they realised that they had responded to the mimic-cry of U Ksuid Tynjang, whom they had often heard described, and against answering whose call they had often been warned.

In a few moments he was with them, and peremptorily he ordered them to rub his itching body with their hands. Although they sickened at the contact, they knew better than to disobey, for U Ksuid Tynjang was known to be very cruel, tickling to death those who dared to disobey him.

It happened that the young brother escaped being seen by the demon, a fact which Ka Thei hoped might turn to their advantage, for she had an alert and a resourceful mind. She motioned to him to squat down on the ground, and she hastily took off the *knup* (leaf umbrella) hanging from her shoulders, and covered him with it.

Soothed by the touch of the young maidens' hands, the *Ksuid* began to dose. With a little contrivance, Ka Thei succeeded in approaching her brother, quickly stuck some shrubs in the *knup*, to make it look like the surrounding jungle, and whispered to him to crawl away as soon as the dawn broke, and seek the path to their village to carry the news of their fate to their parents, and bid them offer sacrifices to the god of Shillong, in whose territory they had been captured, for their deliverance. With the help of the shrub-covered *knup* the boy got away at dawn unobserved, and reached his home, whereupon his parents offered sacrifices to U 'Lei Shillong for the deliverance of their daughters.

Whenever the *Ksuid* fell asleep the sisters were able

to take turns at their unpleasant task. In order to lighten their lot somewhat, they planned to kindle a fire for the following night, and they collected dry sticks and made ready; when night fell they kindled the fire and felt less afraid. During the night, Ka Duh, in putting some fresh wood on the fire, found a large, heavy *dao*—an axe-knife—of iron which she showed to her sister, who at once took it as an augury that deliverance was forthcoming, and that the god of Shillong was working for them. She at once began to think of a plan whereby the *dao* might be useful to break the spell of the demon and to free her sister and herself from his power. She heated the thick blade red-hot while the *Ksuid* slumbered, and, taking it by the handle, she seared his body with the hot iron, so that he died.

Such, however, is the tenacity of all *Ksuids* that, even when they are killed and die, they do not go out of existence. U Ksuid Tynjang could no longer resume the form of a demon as he had formerly done, but he could assume some other form and remain in his old haunts. The form he chose was that of a *jirmi*—a creeper of a tough and tenacious nature which entangles the feet of hunters when they run in the chase, and saps the life out of the forest trees, and destroys the plants cultivated by mankind. This plant is known to this day as the Tynjang creeper.

XIX

WHAT MAKES THE LIGHTNING

In the early days of the world, when the animals fraternised with mankind, they tried to emulate the manners and customs of men, and they spoke their language.

Mankind held a great festival every thirteen moons, where the strongest men and the handsomest youths danced "sword dances" and contested in archery and other noble games, such as befitted their race and their tribe as men of the Hills and the Forests—the oldest and the noblest of all the tribes.

The animals used to attend these festivals and enjoyed watching the games and the dances. Some of the younger and more enterprising among them even clamoured for a similar carnival for the animals, to which, after a time, the elders agreed; so it was decided that the animals should appoint a day to hold a great feast.

After a period of practising dances and learning games, U Pyrthat, the thunder giant, was sent out with his big drum to summon all the world to the festival. The drum of U Pyrthat was the biggest and the loudest of all drums, and could be heard from the most remote corner of the forest; consequently a very large multitude came together, such as had never before been seen at any festival.

The animals were all very smartly arrayed, each one after his or her own taste and fashion, and each one carrying some weapon of warfare or a musical instrument, according to the part he intended to play in the festival. There was much amusement when the squirrel came up, beating on a little drum as he marched; in his wake came the little bird Shakyllia, playing on a flute, followed by the porcupine marching to the rhythm of a pair of small cymbals.

Every one was exceedingly merry—they joked and poked fun at one another, in great glee: some of the animals laughed so much on that feast day that they have never been able to laugh since. The mole was there, and on looking up he saw the owl trying to dance, swaying as if she were drunk, and tumbling against all sorts of obstacles, as she could not see where she was going, at which he laughed so heartily that his eyes became narrow slits and have remained so to this day.

When the merriment was at its height U Kui, the lynx, arrived on the scene, displaying a very handsome silver sword which he had procured at great expense to make a show at the festival. When he began to dance and to brandish the silver sword, everybody applauded. He really danced very gracefully, but so much approbation turned his head, and he became very uplifted, and began to think himself better than all his neighbours.

Just then U Pyrthat, the thunder giant, happened to look round, and he saw the performance of the lynx and admired the beauty of the silver sword, and he asked to have the handling of it for a short time, as a favour, saying that he would like to dance a little, but had brought no instrument except his big drum. This was not at all to U Kui's liking, for he did not want any one but himself to handle his fine weapon; but all the animals began to shout as if with one voice, saying "Shame!" for showing such discourtesy to a guest, and especially to the guest by whose kindly offices the assembly had been summoned together; so U Kui was driven to yield up his silver sword.

As soon as U Pyrthat got possession of the sword he began to wield it with such rapidity and force that it flashed like leaping flame, till all eyes were dazzled almost to blindness, and at the same time he started to beat on his big drum with such violence that the earth shook and trembled and the animals fled in terror to hide in the jungle.

During the confusion U Pyrthat leaped to the sky, taking the lynx's silver sword with him, and he is frequently seen brandishing it wildly there and beating loudly on his drum. In many countries people call these manifestations "thunder" and "lightning," but the Ancient Khasis who were present at the festival knew them to be the stolen sword of the lynx.

U Kui was very disconsolate, and has never grown reconciled to his loss. It is said of him that he has never wandered far from home since then, in order to live near a mound he is trying to raise, which he hopes will one day reach the sky. He hopes to climb to the top of it, to overtake the giant U Pyrthat, and to seize once more his silver sword.

XX

THE PROHIBITED FOOD

When mankind first came to live upon the earth, the Great God saw fit to walk abroad in their midst frequently, and permitted them to hold converse with Him on matters pertaining to their duties and their welfare. At one time the discourse turned on the terrible consequences of disobedience, which caused punishment to fall, not only on the transgressor himself, but upon the entire human race also.

The man could not comprehend the mystery and sought for enlightenment from God, and in order to help him to understand, the Great God said unto him, "Do thou retire for seven days to meditate upon this matter; at the end of the seven days I will again visit the earth; seek me then and we will discourse further. In the meantime go into the forest and hew down the giant tree which I point out to thee, and on thy peril beware of cutting down any other trees." And He pointed out a large tree in the middle of the forest.

Thereupon the Great God ascended into heaven, and the man went forth to meditate and to cut down the giant tree, as he had been commanded.

At the expiration of seven days the man came to the

appointed place and the Great God came to him. He questioned him minutely about his work and his meditations during the week of retirement, but the man had gained no further knowledge nor received any new light. So the Great God, to help him, began to question him. Their discourse was after this manner :

" Hast thou cut down the tree as thou wert commanded ? "

" Behold, its place is empty, I have cut it down."

" Didst thou observe the command in all things ? Didst thou abstain from cutting down any of the other trees ? "

" I abstained from cutting down any other trees ; only the one that was pointed out to me have I cut down."

" What are all these trees and shrubs that I see scattered about ? "

" These were broken and uprooted by the weight of the great tree as it fell."

" Behold, here are some trees that have been cut down with an axe ; how did this happen ? "

" The jungle was so thick I could not reach the giant tree without first cutting a path for myself."

" That is true ; therefore learn from this parable, man is so great that, if he falls into transgression, others must suffer with him."

But the man still marvelled, and his mind remained dark. The Great God, in His long-sufferance, told him to ponder further upon the parable of the giant tree. So the Great God walked abroad for a time and man was left alone to ponder. When He returned He found the man still puzzled and unable to comprehend ; and once again He questioned him.

"What took place in My absence?"

"Nothing of importance that I can think of."

"Why didst thou cry out as if in pain?"

"It was for a very trivial cause; an ant bit me in my heel."

"And what didst thou do?"

"I took a stone and killed the ant and the whole nest of ants."

"This also is a parable; because one ant bit thee the whole nest was destroyed. Man is the ant; if man transgresseth he and all his race must suffer."

Yet the man comprehended not: whereupon the Great God granted him another seven days to retire and to meditate upon the parables of the giant tree and the ant.

Again the man came to the appointed place at the end of seven days' seeking to receive fuller knowledge and understanding. The Great God had not yet appeared, so the man took a walk in the forest to await His coming. As he wandered aimlessly about, he met a stranger carrying a small net in his hand out of which he was eating some food. Now this stranger was a demon, but the man did not know it.

"Where art thou going?" asked the stranger affably after the manner of the country.

"Just to walk for my pleasure," replied the man; "what food art thou eating?"

"Only some cakes of bread which I find very tasty; take some and eat." And he passed the net to him.

"Thy offer is kindly made, but do not take it amiss that I refuse to accept thy bread, for it is decreed that we shall live on rice alone."

"Even so, but surely to take a morsel to taste would not be wrong."

This time the man did not resist, but accepted a cake of bread and ate it with enjoyment, after which the stranger departed, taking his bag of cakes with him.

The man had scarcely swallowed the strange food when he heard the voice of the Great God calling unto him from the skies, saying:

"What hast thou done, oh man? Thou knowest the decree that rice was provided to be thy food, yet thou hast unmindfully transgressed and partaken of the strange food of the tempter. Henceforth thou and thy race shall be tormented by the strange being whose food thou hast eaten. By eating his food thou hast given him dominion over thee and over thy race, and to escape from his torments thou and thy race must give of thy substance to appease him and to avert his wrath."

Thus, too late, the man began to understand, and ever since then the days of men have been full of sorrow because man yielded to the tempter's voice instead of submitting to the decrees of the Great God.

XXI

THE COOING OF THE DOVES

Of all the birds there are none that keep themselves more separate than the doves. They do not peck at other birds as the crows and the vultures do, but, on restless foot and wing, they quickly withdraw themselves from every presuming neighbour.

The Ancient Khasis say that at one time the doves sang like other birds, and the following story tells how they ceased their singing and came to express their feelings in the plaintive "Coo-oo" for which they are noted throughout the world.

Once a family of doves lived very happily in the forest, and its youngest member was a beautiful female called Ka Paro. Her parents and all the family were very indulgent to her, and never permitted her to risk the danger of the grain-fields until they had ascertained that there were no hunters or wild beasts likely to attack her; so Ka Paro used to stay in the shelter of her home until they gave a signal that the land was safe and clear.

One day, while waiting for the signal, she happened to go up into a tall tree on which there were clusters of luscious red berries growing. As the doves usually subsisted on grain, Ka Paro did not pay much attention to the berries; she sat on a branch, preening her feathers and watching other birds who came to pick them.

By and by there came a smart young Jylleit (a jungle bird with gorgeous green and gold feathers) who perched to pick berries upon the very branch on which Ka Paro sat. She had never seen such a beautiful bird, and to please him she sang to him one of her sweetest songs. U Jylleit was quickly attracted by the sweet voice and the gentle manners of the dove, and a pleasant intimacy grew between the two. Ka Paro came to that tree to preen her feathers and to sing every day, while the Jylleit admired her and picked the berries.

After a time U Jylleit sent to the dove's parents to ask her in marriage. Although their young daughter pressed them hard to give their consent, the parents were wise, and did not want to trust the happiness of their pet child to a stranger until they had time to test his worth; they knew too that marriages between alien tribes were scarcely ever a success. So, to test the constancy of the young suitor, they postponed the marriage till the winter, and with that the lovers had to be content. The parents remembered that the berries would be over by the winter, and it remained to be seen whether the Jylleit would be willing to forgo his luxuries and to share the frugal food of the doves, or whether he would fly away to some other forests where berries were to be found. Ka Paro was so much in love that she was very confident of the fidelity of her suitor, but to her sorrow, as soon as the berries were finished, U Jylleit flitted away without even a word of farewell, and she never saw him again.

From that time Ka Paro ceased to sing. She could only utter the longing and sorrow that was in her heart in sad and plaintive notes, so the doves are cooing sadly even in their happiest moments.

XXII

HOW THE MONKEY'S COLOUR BECAME GREY

In olden times the monkeys had long hair of different colours covering their bodies, and they were much more handsome than they are in the present day. They were very inquisitive animals and liked to meddle in the affairs of other people, and they caused a lot of trouble in the world.

One day a monkey wandering on the plains met Ram, the god of the Hindus, searching for the goddess Sita. Ram, thinking that the monkey by his inquisitiveness and audacity might help to find her, bribed him to come to his service.

After making enquiries far and near, the monkey heard at last that Ka Sita was confined in a fort in the island of Ceylon, so he went and told the god Ram. Thereupon Ram gathered together a great host to go and fight the king of the island of Ceylon, but they found the place infested with dragons and goblins of the most hostile disposition, so that they dared not venture to land.

The hosts of Ram then held a consultation, and they decided that, as the monkey had been the cause of their coming there, he must find out a way for them to land without being destroyed by the dragons. The monkey, not knowing what to say, suggested that they should burn down the forests of Ceylon so that the dragons could have no place to hide.

Upon this the hosts of Ram declared that the monkey himself must go over to put his plan into execution. So they dipped a long piece of cloth in oil and tied one end of it to the monkey's tail and set fire to the other end of it, and the monkey went over to the island and ran hither and thither dragging the flaming cloth behind him and setting the forests on fire everywhere he went, until all the forests of Ceylon were in flames.

Before he could get back to his companions he saw with dismay that the cloth was nearly burnt out, and the heat from the fire behind him began to singe his long hair; whereupon, fearing to be burnt alive, he plunged into the sea and the flames were extinguished. From that time the monkey's hair has been grey and short as a sign that he once set the forests of Ceylon on fire.

XXIII

THE LEGEND OF KA PANSHANDI, THE LAZY TORTOISE

Once upon a time there lived a young tortoise near a large pool. She was very ill-favoured and ugly in appearance and very foolish, as well as being of a lazy disposition, and, like all lazy people, she was slovenly and dirty in her habits. Her name was Ka Panshandi.

The pool near which she lived being very clear, the stars and other heavenly bodies often gazed into it to behold their own images. At times the reflection of countless shining, blinking stars would be visible in the placid waters till the pool looked like a little part of the sky. At such times Ka Panshandi took immense delight in plunging into the pool, darting backwards and forwards and twirling round the bright silvery spots with great glee and contentment.

Among those who came frequently to gaze at themselves in the pool was U Lurmangkhara, the brightest of all the stars; he began to notice the playful gambols of Ka Panshandi in the water and to admire her twirling motions. He lived so far away that he could not see her ugliness, nor could he know that she was lazy and foolish. All he knew was that she exposed herself nightly to the chilly waters of the pool in order (as he thought) to have the pleasure of being near the images of the stars, which was very flattering to his vanity. If she was so strongly attracted by their images, he thought to himself, how much more would she adore the real live stars if she were brought into contact with them.

U Lurmangkhara fell deeply in love with her, and determined to go down to the earth to marry her and to endow her with all his wealth, for he was very rich and had always lived in great splendour.

When his relations and friends heard of his purpose, they were much disturbed, and they came to remonstrate with him against what they considered to be a very rash and risky step—to go to a foreign land to make his home and to mate with an unknown consort whose habits and outlook on life might be altogether alien to him. But U Lurmangkhara would listen to no counsel. Persons in love never take heed of other people's advice. Down to the earth he came, and there married Ka Panshandi and endowed her with all his wealth.

When Ka Panshandi found herself a rich wife, having unexpectedly won one of the noblest husbands in the world, her vanity knew no bounds, and she grew more indolent and idle than ever. Her house was squalid, and she minded not when even her own body was daubed with mud, and she felt no shame to see her husband's meals served off unscoured platters. U Lurmangkhara was very disappointed; being patient and gentle, he tried by kind words to teach his wife to amend her ways, but it was of no avail. Gradually he grew discontented and spoke angrily to her, but she remained as callous and as indifferent as ever, for it is easier to turn even a thief from stealing than to induce a sluggard to renounce his sloth. He threatened to leave her, her neighbours also repeatedly warned her that she would lose her good husband unless she altered her ways, but she remained as unconcerned as ever. At last, driven to despair, U Lurmangkhara gathered together all his wealth and went back to his home in the sky.

Ka Panshandi was filled with remorse and grief when she found that her husband had departed. She called piteously after him, promising to reform if he would only return, but it was too late. He never came back, and she was left to her squalor and her shame.

To this day Ka Panshandi is still hoping to see U Lurmangkhara coming back to the earth, and she is seen crawling about mournfully, with her neck outstretched towards the sky in expectation of his coming, but there is no sign of his return, and her life is dull and joyless.

After these events Ka Panshandi's name became a mockery and a proverb in the land; ballads were sung setting forth her fate as a warning to lazy and thriftless wives. To the present day a forsaken wife who entertains hope of her husband's return is likened by the Khasis to Ka Panshandi in her expectant attitude with her head lifted above her shell: "*Ka Panshandi dem-lor-khah.*"

XXIV

THE IDIOT AND THE HYNDET BREAD

Long, long ago there lived on the Khasi Hills a certain widow with her only son, a lad possessed of great personal beauty, who was mentally deficient, and was known in the village as "U Bieit" (the idiot).

The mother, being very poor and having neither kith nor kin to help her, was obliged to go out to work every day to support herself and her hapless child, so he was left to his own devices, roaming at large in the village. In this way he grew up to be very troublesome to his neighbours, for he often broke into their houses to forage for something to eat and caused much damage and loss.

Like most people of weak intellect, U Bieit showed wonderful cunning in some directions, especially in the matter of procuring some good thing to eat, and the way he succeeded in duping some of his more sagacious comrades in order to obtain some dainty tit-bits of food was a matter of much amusement and merriment. But there were so many unpleasant incidents that people could not safely leave their houses, and matters at last became so serious that the widow was ordered to leave the village on his account.

She sought admission into many of the surrounding

villages, but the fame of U Bieit had travelled before him and no one was willing to let them dwell in their midst. So in great distress she took him down to the plains, where there was a big river along which many boats used to sail. Here she mournfully determined to abandon him, hoping that some of the wealthy merchants who often passed that way might be attracted by his good looks and take him into their company. She gave him some rice cakes to eat when he should be hungry, and told him to be a good boy and stay by the river-side, and she would bring him more cakes next day.

The boy thoroughly appreciated the promise of more cakes, so was quite willing to be left by the river, but he felt lonely and uncomfortable in his strange surroundings after his mother had gone, and whenever a boat came in sight he ran into the thickets to hide. By and by a large boat was seen approaching with great white sails, which frightened him greatly and sent him running into a thicket with all his might. It happened that a wealthy merchant was returning from a journey, and landed to take food close to the hiding-place of U Bieit. The servants were going backward and forward into the boat while preparing their master's food, and, fearing lest some of them might tamper with his chest of gold nuggets, he ordered them to carry it ashore, and buried it in the sands close to where he sat.

Just as he finished his repast a heavy shower came on, and the merchant hurried to the shelter of his boat; in his haste he forgot all about the chest of gold buried in the sands, and the boat sailed away without it.

All this time the idiot boy was watching the proceedings with great curiosity and a longing to share the tempting meal, but fear of the boat with white sails kept him from showing himself. However, as soon as the boat was out of sight, he came out of the thicket and began to unearth the buried chest. When he saw the gold nuggets he thought they were some kind of cakes, and, putting one in his mouth, he tried to eat it. Finding it so hard, he decided that it must have been unbaked, and his poor marred mind flew at once to his mother, who always baked food for him at home, and, taking the heavy chest on his back, he started through the forest to seek her, and his instinct, like that of a homing pigeon, brought him safely to his mother's door.

It was quite dark when he reached the village, so that nobody saw him, but his mother was awake crying and lamenting her own hard fate which had driven her to desert her unfortunate child. As she cried she kept saying to herself that if only she possessed money she could have obtained the goodwill of her neighbours and been permitted to live with her boy in the village. She was surprised to hear sounds of shuffling at her door resembling the shuffling of her forsaken boy; she got up hurriedly to see who it was, and was relieved and joyful to find him come back to her alive.

She marvelled when she saw him carrying a heavy chest on his shoulders, and she could get but little light from his incoherent speech as to how he had obtained possession of it, but her eyes glittered with delight when she saw that it was full of gold nuggets. She allowed the lad to keep his delusion that they were cakes, and to pacify him she took some rice and made some savoury cakes for him, pretending that she was baking the strange cakes from the chest. After eating these, he went to sleep satisfied and happy.

Now the widow had been longing for gold all her life long, saying that she wanted it to provide better comforts for the son who could not look after himself, but the moment the gold came into her possession her heart was filled with greed. Not only was she not willing to part with any of the nuggets to obtain the favour of the villagers for her son, but she was planning to send him abroad again to search for more gold, regardless of the perils to which he would be exposed. She called him up before daybreak, and, giving him some rice cakes in a bag, she told him to go again to the river-side and to bring home more boxes of cakes for her to bake.

So the boy started out on his fruitless errand, but soon lost his way in the jungle; he could find the path neither to the river nor to his mother's house, so he wandered about disconsolate and hungry in the dense woods, searching for hidden chests and unbaked cakes.

In that forest many fairies had their haunts, but they were invisible to mankind. They knew all about the idiot boy and his sad history, and a great pity welled up in their hearts when they saw how the lust for gold had so corrupted his mother's feelings that she sent him alone and unprotected into the dangers of that great forest. They determined to try and induce him to accompany them to the land of the fairies, where he would be guarded from all harm and where willing hands would minister to all his wants.

So seven of the fairies transformed themselves into the likeness of mankind and put on strong wings like the wings of great eagles, and came to meet U Bieit in the jungle. By this he had become exhausted with want of food, and as soon as he saw the fairies he called out eagerly to ask if they had any food, to which they replied that they had only some *Hyndet bread* (*kpu Hyndet*) which had been baked by the fairies in heaven; and when they gave him some of it, he ate it ravenously and held out his hand for more. This was just what the fairies wanted, for no human being can be taken to fairyland except of his own free will. So they said that they had no more to give in that place, but if he liked to come with them to the land of the fairies beyond the Blue Realm, he could have abundance of choice food and Hyndet cakes. He expressed his readiness to go at once, and asked them how he should get there. They told him to take hold of their wings, to cling firmly, and not to talk on the way; so he took hold of the wings of the fairies and the ascent to fairyland began.

Now as they flew upwards there were many beautiful sights which gave the fairies great delight as they passed. They saw the glories of the highest mountains, and the endless expanse of forest and waters, and the fleeting shadows of the clouds, and the brilliant colours of the rainbow, dazzling in their transient beauty. But the idiot boy saw nothing of these things; his simple mind was absorbed in the one thought—food. When they had ascended to a great height and the borders of fairyland came into view, U Bieit could no longer repress his curiosity, and, forgetting all about the caution not to speak, he asked the fairies eagerly, "Will the Hyndet cakes be big?" As soon as he uttered the words he lost his hold on the fairies' wings and, falling to the earth with great velocity, he died.

The Khasis relate this story mainly as a warning not to impose responsible duties on persons incapable of performing them, and not to raise people into high positions which they are not fitted to fill.

XXV

U RAMHAH

WHERE is the country without its giant-story?

All through the ages the world has revelled in tales of the incomparable prowess and the unrivalled strength and stature of great and distinguished men whom we have learned to call giants. We trace them from the days of Samson and Goliath, past the Knights of Arthur in the "Island of the Mighty" and the great warriors of ancient Greece, down to the mythland of our nursery days, where the exploits of the famous "Jack" and his confederates filled us with wonder and awe. Our world has been a world full of mighty men to whom all the nations pay tribute, and the Khasis in their small corner are not behind the rest of the world in this respect, for they also have on record the exploits of a giant whose fate was as strange as that of any famous giant in history.

The name of the Khasi giant was U Ramhah. He lived in a dark age, and his vision was limited, but according to his lights and the requirements of his country and his generation, he performed great and wonderful feats, such as are performed by all orthodox giants all the world over. He lifted great boulders, he erected huge pillars, he uprooted large trees, he fought wild beasts, he trampled on dragons, he overcame armed hosts single-handed, he championed the cause of the defenceless, and won for himself praise and renown.

When his fame was at its height he smirched his reputation by his bad actions. After the great victory over U Thlen in the cave of Pomdoloi, he became very uplifted and proud, and considered himself entitled to the possessions of the Khasis. So instead of helping and defending his neighbours as of yore, he began to oppress and to plunder them, and came to be regarded as a notorious highwayman, to be avoided and dreaded, who committed thefts and crimes wherever he went.

At this period he is described as a very tall and powerful man whose stature reached "half way to the sky," and he always carried a *soop* (a large basket of plaited bamboo) on his back, into which he put all his spoils, which were generally some articles of food or clothing. He broke into houses, looted the markets and waylaid travellers. The plundered people used to run after him, clinging to his big *soop*, but he used to beat them and sometimes kill them, and by reason of his great strength and long strides he always got away with his booty, leaving havoc and devastation behind him. He was so strong and so terrible that no one could check his crimes or impose any punishments.

There lived in the village of Cherra in those days a wealthy woman called Ka Bthuh, who had suffered much and often at the hands of U Ramhah, and whose anger against him burnt red-hot. She had pleaded urgently with the men of her village to rise in a body to avenge her wrongs, but they always said that it was useless. Whenever she met U Ramhah she insulted him by pointing and shaking her finger at him, saying, "You may conquer the strength of a man, but beware of the cunning of a woman." For this saying U Ramhah hated her, for it showed that he had not been able to overawe her as everybody else had been overawed by him, and he raided her godowns more frequently than ever, not dreaming that she was scheming to defeat him.

One day Ka Bthuh made a great feast; she sent invitations to many villages far and near, for she wanted it to be as publicly known as possible in order to lure U Ramhah to attend. It was one of his rude habits to go uninvited to feasts and to gobble up all the eatables before the invited guests had been helped.

The day of Ka Bthuh's feast came and many guests arrived, but before the rice had been distributed there was a loud cry that U Ramhah was marching towards the village. Everybody considered this very annoying, but Ka Bthuh, the hostess, pretended not to be disturbed, and told the people to let the giant eat as much as he liked first, and she would see that they were all helped later on. At this U Ramhah laughed, thinking that she was beginning to be afraid of him, and he helped himself freely to the cooked rice and curry that was at hand. He always ate large mouthfuls, but at feast times he used to put an even greater quantity of rice into his mouth, just to make an impression and a show. Ka Bthuh had anticipated all this, and she stealthily put into the rice some sharp steel blades which the giant swallowed unsuspectingly.

When he had eaten to his full content U Ramhah took his departure, and when he had gone out of earshot Ka Bthuh told the people what she had done. They marvelled much at her cunning, and they all said it was a just deed to punish one whose crimes were so numerous and so flagrant, but who escaped penalty by reason of his great strength. From that time Ka Bthuh won great praise and became famous.

U Ramhah never reached his home from that feast. The sharp blades he had swallowed cut his intestines and he died on the hill-side alone and unattended, as the wild animals die, and there was no one to regret his death.

When the members of his clan heard of his death they came in a great company to perform rites and to cremate his body, but the body was so big that it could not be cremated, and so they decided to leave it till the flesh rotted, and to come again to gather together his bones. After a long time they came to gather the bones, but it was found that there was no urn large enough to contain them, so they piled them together on the hill-side until a large urn could be made.

While the making of the large urn was in progress there arose a great storm, and a wild hurricane blew from the north, which carried away the bleached bones of U Ramhah, and scattered them all over the south borders of the Khasi Hills, where they remain to this day in the form of lime-rocks, the many winding caves and crevices of which are said to be the cavities in the marrowless bones of the giant. Thus U Ramhah, who injured and plundered the Khasis in his life-time, became the source of inestimable wealth to them after his death.

His name is heard on every hearth, used as a proverb to describe objects of abnormal size or people of abnormal strength.

XXVI

HOW THE CAT CAME TO LIVE WITH MAN

In olden times Ka Miaw, the cat, lived in the jungle with her brother the tiger, who was king of the jungle. She was very proud of her high pedigree and anxious to display the family greatness, and to live luxuriously according to the manner of families of high degree; but the tiger, although he was very famous abroad, was not at all mindful of the well-being and condition of his family, and allowed them to be often in want. He himself, by his skill and great prowess, obtained the most delicate morsels for his own consumption, but as it involved trouble to bring booty home for his household, he preferred to leave what he did not want himself to rot on the roadside, or to be eaten by any chance scavenger. Therefore, the royal larder was often very bare and empty.

Thus the cat was reduced to great privations, but so jealous was she for the honour and good name of her house that, to hide her poverty from her friends and neighbours, she used to sneak out at night-time, when nobody could see her, in order to catch mice and frogs and other common vermin for food.

Once she ventured to speak to her brother on the matter, asking him what glory there was in being king if his family were obliged to work and to fare like common folks. The tiger was so angered that she never dared to approach the subject again, and she continued to live her hard life and to shield the family honour.

One day the tiger was unwell, and a number of his neighbours came to enquire after his health. Desiring to entertain them with tobacco, according to custom, he shouted to his sister to light the hookah and to serve it round to the company. Now, even in the most ordinary household, it is very contrary to good breeding to order the daughter of the house to serve the hookah, and Ka Miaw felt the disgrace keenly, and, hoping to excuse herself, she answered that there was no fire left by which to light the hookah. This answer displeased the tiger greatly, for he felt that his authority was being flouted before his friends He ordered his sister angrily to go to the dwelling of mankind to fetch a firebrand with which to light the hookah, and, fearing to be punished if she disobeyed, the cat ran off as she was bidden and came to the dwelling of mankind.

Some little children were playing in the village, and when they saw Ka Miaw they began to speak gently to her and to stroke her fur. This was so pleasant to her feelings after the harsh treatment from her brother that she forgot all about the firebrand and stayed to play with the children, purring to show her pleasure.

Meanwhile the tiger and his friends sat waiting impatiently for the hookah that never came. It was considered a great privilege to draw a whiff from the royal hookah; but seeing that the cat delayed her return, the visitors took their departure, and showed a little sullenness at not receiving any mark of hospitality in their king's house.

The tiger's anger against his sister was very violent, and, regardless of his ill-health, he went out in search of her. Ka Miaw heard him coming, and knew from his growl that he was angry; she suddenly remembered her forgotten errand, and, hastily snatching a firebrand from the hearth, she started for home.

Her brother met her on the way and began to abuse her, threatening to beat her, upon which she threw down the firebrand at his feet in her fright and ran back to the abode of mankind, where she has remained ever since, supporting herself as of old by catching frogs and mice, and purring to the touch of little children.

XXVII

HOW THE FOX GOT HIS WHITE BREAST

ONCE a fox, whose name was U Myrsiang, lived in a cave near the residence of a Siem (Chief). This fox was a very shameless marauder, and had the impudence to conduct his raids right into the Siem's private barn-yard, and to devour the best of his flocks, causing him much annoyance and loss.

The Siem gave his servants orders to catch U Myrsiang, but though they laid many traps and snares in his way he was so wily and so full of cunning that he managed to evade every pitfall, and to continue his raids on the Siem's flocks.

One of the servants, more ingenious than his fellows, suggested that they should bring out the iron cage in which the Siem was wont to lock up state criminals, and try and wheedle the fox into entering it. So they brought out the iron cage and set it open near the entrance to the barn-yard, with a man on guard to watch.

By and by, U Myrsiang came walking by very cautiously, sniffing the air guardedly to try and discover if any hidden dangers lay in his path. He soon reached the cage, but it aroused no suspicion in him, for it was so large and so unlike every trap he was familiar with that he entered it without a thought of peril, and ere he was aware of his error, the man on guard had bolted the door behind him and made him a prisoner.

There was great jubilation in the Siem's household when the capture of the fox was made known. The Siem himself was so pleased that he commanded his servants to prepare a feast on the following day as a reward for their vigilance and ingenuity. He also gave orders not to kill the fox till the next day, and that he should be brought out of the cage after the feast and executed in a public place as a warning to other thieves and robbers. So U Myrsiang was left to pine in his prison for that night.

The fox was very unhappy, as all people in confinement must be. He explored the cage from end to end but found no passage of egress. He thought out many plans of escape, but not one of them could be put into execution, and he was driven to face the doom of certain death. He whined in his misery and despair, and roamed about the cage all night.

Some time towards morning he was disturbed by the sounds of footsteps outside his cage, and, thinking that the Siem's men had come to kill him, he lay very still, hardly venturing to breathe. To his relief the new-comer turned out to be a belated traveller, who, upon seeing a cage, sat down, leaning his weary body against the bars, while U Myrsiang kept very still, not wishing to disclose his presence until he found out something more about his unexpected companion, and hoping also to turn his coming to some good account.

The traveller was an outlaw driven away from a neighbouring state for some offence, and was in great perplexity how to procure the permission of the Siem (into whose state he had now wandered) to dwell there and be allowed to cultivate the land. Thinking that he was quite alone, he began to talk to himself, not knowing that a wily fox was listening attentively to all that he was saying.

"I am a most unfortunate individual," said the stranger. "I have been driven away from my home and people, I have no money and no friends, and no belongings except this little polished mirror which no one is likely to buy. I am so exhausted that if they drive me out of this State again I shall die of starvation on the roadside. If I could only find a friend who could help me to win the favour of the Siem, so that I may be permitted to live here unmolested for a time, till my trouble blows over!"

U Myrsiang's heart was beating very fast with renewed hope when he heard these words, and he tried to think of some way to delude the stranger to imagine that he was some one who had influence with the Siem, and to get the man to open the cage and let him out. So with all the cunning he was capable of, he accosted the man in his most affable and courteous manner:

"Friend and brother," he said, "do not despair. I think I can put you in the way, not only to win the Siem's favour, but to become a member of his family."

The outlaw was greatly embarrassed when he discovered that some one had overheard him talking. It was such a dark night he could not see the fox, but thought that it was a fellow-man who had accosted him. Fearing to commit himself further if he talked about himself, he tried to divert the conversation away from himself, and asked his companion who he was and what he was doing alone in the cage at night.

The fox, nothing loth to monopolise the conversation,

gave a most plausible account of his misfortunes, and his tale seemed so sincere and apparently true that it convinced the man on the instant.

"There is great trouble in this State," said U Myrsiang. "The only daughter of the Siem is sick, and according to the divinations she is likely to die unless she can be wedded before sunset to-morrow, and her bridegroom must be a native of some other State. The time was too short to send envoys to any of the neighbouring States to arrange for the marriage, and as I happened to pass this way on a journey, the Siem's men forcibly detained me, on finding that I was a foreigner, and to-morrow they will compel me to marry the Siem's daughter, which is much against my will. If you open the door of this cage and let me out, you may become the Siem's son-in-law by taking my place in the cage."

"What manner of man are you," asked the outlaw, "that you should disdain the honour of marrying the daughter of a Siem?"

"You are mistaken to think that I disdain the honour," said the fox. "If I had been single I should have rejoiced in the privilege, but I am married already, and have a wife and family in my own village far from here, and my desire is to be released so that I may return to them."

"In that case," replied the man, "I think you are right to refuse, but as for me it will be a most desirable union, and I shall be only too glad to exchange places with you."

Thereupon he opened the door of the cage and went in, while U Myrsiang slipped out, and bolted the door behind him.

The man was so pleased with his seeming good fortune

that at parting he took off his polished mirror which was suspended round his neck by a silver chain, and begged his companion to accept it in remembrance of their short but strange encounter. As he was handing it to U Myrsiang, his hand came into contact with the fox's thick fur, and he realised then that he had been duped, and had, owing to his credulity, released the most thieving rogue in the forest. Regrets were vain. He was firmly imprisoned within the cage, while he heard the laughter of U Myrsiang echoing in the distance as he hurried away to safety, taking the polished mirror with him.

The fox was well aware that it was unsafe for him to remain any longer in that locality, so, after fastening the mirror firmly round his neck, he hastened away with all speed, and did not halt till he came to a remote and secluded part of the jungle, where he stopped to take his breath and to rest.

Unknown to U Myrsiang, a big tiger was lying in wait for prey in that part of the jungle, and, upon seeing the fox, made ready to spring upon him. But the fox, hearing some noise, turned round suddenly, and by that movement the polished mirror came right in front of the tiger's face. The tiger saw in it the reflection of his own big jaws and flaming eyes, from which he slunk away in terror, thinking that U Myrsiang was some great tiger-demon haunting the jungle in the shape of a fox, and from that time the tiger has never been known to attack the fox.

One day, when hotly pursued by hunters, the fox plunged into a deep river. As he swam across, the flood carried away his polished mirror, but the stamp of it remains to this day on his breast in the form of a patch of white fur.

XXVIII

HOW THE TIGER GOT HIS STRENGTH

AFTER the animals were created they were sent to live in the jungle, but they were so foolish that they got into one another's way and interfered one with another and caused much inconvenience in the world. In order to produce better order, the *Bleis* (gods) called together a Durbar to decide on the different qualities with which it would be well to endow the animals, so as to make them intelligent and able to live in harmony with one another. After this, mankind and all the animals were summoned to the presence of the *Bleis*, and each one was given such intelligence and sense as seemed best to suit his might and disposition: the man received beauty and wisdom, and to the tiger were given craftiness and the power to walk silently.

When the man returned to his kindred, and his mother beheld him, her heart was lifted with pride, for she knew that the *Bleis* had given to him the best of their gifts, and that henceforth all the animals would be inferior to him in beauty and intelligence. Realising with regret that he had not received physical strength equal to the beauty of his person, and that consequently his life would be always in danger, she told her son to go back to the *Bleis* to ask for the gift of strength.

The man went back to the *Bleis* according to the command of his mother, but it was so late when he arrived that the *Bleis* were about to retire. Seeing that he was comelier than any of the animals and possessed more wisdom, which made him worthy of the gift of strength, they told him to come on the morrow and they would bestow upon him the desired gift. The man was dismissed till the following day, but he went away happy in his mind, knowing that the *Bleis* would not go back on their word.

Now it happened that the tiger was roaming about in that vicinity, and by reason of his silent tread he managed to come unobserved near enough to hear the *Bleis* and the man talking about the gift of strength. He determined to forestall the man on the morrow, and to obtain the gift of strength for himself; soon he slunk away lest it should be discovered that he had been listening.

Early on the following morning, before the *Bleis* had come forth from their retirement, the tiger went to their abode and sent in a messenger to say that he had come according to their command to obtain the gift of strength, upon which the *Bleis* endowed him with strength twelve times greater than what he had before possessed, thinking that they were bestowing it upon the man.

The tiger felt himself growing strong, and as soon as he left the abode of the *Bleis*, he leaped forward twelve strides, and twelve strides upward, and so strong was he that it was unto him but as one short stride. Then he knew that he had truly forestalled the man, and had obtained the gift of strength, and could overcome men in battle.

Later in the day, in accordance with the command he had received, the man set out for the abode of the *Bleis*, but on the way the tiger met him and challenged him to fight, and began to leap and bound upwards and forwards to show how strong he was, and said that he had received the "twelve strengths" and no one would be able to withstand him. He was just about to spring when the man evaded him, and ran away towards the abode of the *Bleis*. When he came there and presented himself before them, they asked him angrily, "Why dost thou come again to trouble us? We have already given thee the gift of strength." Then the man knew that the tiger's boast was true, and he told the *Bleis* of his encounter with the tiger on the way, and of his boast that he had obtained the gift of strength. They were greatly annoyed that deception had been practised on them, but there is no decree by which to recall a gift when once it has been bestowed by the *Bleis*. They looked upon the man with pity, and said that one so beautiful and full of wisdom should not be left defenceless at the mercy of the inferior animals. So they gave unto him a bow and an arrow, and told him, "When the tiger attacks thee with his strength, shoot, and the arrow will pierce his body and kill him. Behold, we have given to thee the gift of skill to make and to use weapons of warfare whereby thou wilt be able to combat the lower animals."

Thus the tiger received strength, and man received the gift of skill. The mother of mankind, when she saw it, told her sons to abstain from using their weapons against one another, but to turn them against the animals only, according to the decree of the *Bleis*.

XXIX

WHY THE GOAT LIVES WITH MANKIND

In early times the goat lived in the jungle, leading a free and independent life, like all the other animals. The following story gives an account of her flight from the animals to make her dwelling with Man.

One fine spring day, when the young leaves were sprouting on the forest trees, Ka Blang, the goat, went out in search of food. Her appetite was sharpened by the delicious smell of the spring, which filled the air and the forest, so, not being satisfied with grass, she began to pluck the green leaves from a bush. While she was busy plucking and eating, she was startled to hear the deep growl of the tiger close beside her.

The tiger asked her angrily, "What art thou doing there ?"

Ka Blang was so upset by this sudden interruption, and in such fear of the big and ferocious beast, that she began to tremble from head to foot, so that even her beard shook violently, and she hardly knew what she was doing or saying. In her fright she quavered :

"I am eating *khla*" (a tiger), instead of saying, "I am eating *sla*" (leaves).

The tiger took this answer for insolence and became very angry. He was preparing to spring upon her when he caught sight of her shaking beard, which appeared to him like the tuft of hair on a warrior's lance when it is lifted against an enemy. He thought that Ka Blang must be some powerful and savage beast able to attack him, and he ran away from her in terror.

Now Ka Blang, having an ungrateful heart, instead of being thankful for her deliverance, grew discontented with her lot, and began to grumble because she had not been endowed with the strength attributed to her by the tiger, and she went about bewailing her inferiority.

One day, in her wanderings, she climbed to the top of an overhanging cliff, and there she lay down to chew the cud, and, as usual, to dwell on her grievances. It happened that the tiger was again prowling in the same vicinity, but when he saw the goat approaching he fled in fear, and hid himself under the very cliff on to which she had climbed. There he lay very still, for fear of betraying his presence to the goat, for he was still under the delusion that she was a formidable and mighty animal. Ka Blang, all unconscious of his presence, began to grumble aloud, saying:

"I am the poorest and the weakest of all the beasts, without any means of defence or strength to withstand an attack. I have neither tusks nor claws to make an enemy fear me. It is true that the tiger once ran away from me because he mistook my beard for a sign of strength; but if he had only known the truth he would have killed me on the instant, for even a small dog could kill me if he clutched me by the throat."

The tiger, beneath the rock, was listening to every word, and, as he listened, his wrath was greatly kindled to find that he had disgraced himself by running away from such a contemptible creature, and he determined now to avenge himself for that humiliation. He crept stealthily from his hiding-place, and, ere she was aware of his approach, Ka Blang was clutched by the throat and killed.

In order to restore his prestige, the tiger proclaimed far and wide how he had captured and killed the goat, and after that other tigers and savage beasts began to hunt the goats, and there followed such a general slaughter of goats that they were nearly exterminated.

Driven to great extremity, the few remaining goats held a tribal council to consider how to save themselves from the onslaughts of the tigers, but, finding themselves powerless to offer any resistance, they determined to apply to mankind for protection. When they came to him, Man said that he could not come to the jungle to defend them, but they must come and live in his village if they wished to be protected by him. So the goats ran away from the jungle for ever, and came to live with mankind.

XXX

HOW THE OX CAME TO BE THE SERVANT OF MAN

When mankind first came to live upon the earth, they committed many blunders, for they were ignorant and wasteful, not knowing how to shift for themselves, and having no one to teach them. The Deity who was watching their destinies saw their misfortunes and pitied them, for he saw that unless their wastefulness ceased they would perish of want when they multiplied and became numerous in the world. So the Deity called to him the ox, who was a strong and patient animal, and sent him as a messenger to mankind, to bless them, and to show them how to prosper.

The ox had to travel a long way in the heat, and was much worried by the flies that swarmed round his path and the small insects that clung to his body and sucked his blood. Then a crow alighted on his back and began to peck at the insects, upon which it loved to feed; this eased the ox greatly, and he was very pleased to see the crow, and he told her where he was going, as a messenger from the Deity to mankind.

The crow was very interested when she heard this, and questioned him minutely about the message he had been sent to deliver, and the ox told her all that he had been commanded to say to mankind—how he was to give them the blessing of the Deity and to warn them not to waste the products of the earth lest they died of want. They must learn to be thrifty and careful so that they might live to be old and wise, and they were to boil only sufficient rice for each meal, so as not to waste their food.

When the crow heard this she was much disturbed, for she saw that there would be no leavings for the crows if mankind followed these injunctions. So she said to the ox, "Will you repay my kindness to you in destroying the insects that worry you by giving a message like that to mankind to deprive me of my accustomed spoil?" She begged of him to teach mankind to cook much rice always, and to ordain many ceremonies to honour their dead ancestors by offering rice to the gods, so that the crows and the other birds might have abundance to eat. Thus, because she had eased his torments, the ox listened to her words, and when he came to mankind he delivered only part of the message of the Deity, and part of the message of the crow.

When the time came for the ox to return, a great fear overcame him as he approached the abode of the Deity, for he saw that he had greatly trespassed and that the Deity would be wrathful. In the hope of obtaining forgiveness, he at once confessed his wrongdoing, how he had been tempted by the crow, and had delivered the wrong message. This confession did not mitigate the anger of the Deity, for he arose, and, with great fury, he struck the ox such a blow on the mouth that all his upper teeth fell out, and another blow behind the ribs which made a great hollow there, and he drove the disobedient animal from his presence, to seek pasture and shelter wherever he could find them.

After this the ox came back sorrowfully to mankind, and for food and for shelter he offered to become their servant; and, because he was strong and patient, mankind allowed him to become their servant.

Ever since he was struck by the Deity the ox has had no teeth in the upper jaw, and the hollow behind his ribs remains to this day; it can never be filled up, however much grass and grain he eats, for it is the mark of the fist of the Deity.

XXXI

THE LOST BOOK

AFTER mankind began to multiply on the earth and had become numerous, and scattered into many regions, they lost much of their knowledge of the laws of God, and in their ignorance they committed many mistakes in their mode of worship, each one worshipping in his own way after his own fancy, without regard to what was proper and acceptable in the sight of God.

In order to restore their knowledge and to reform their mode of worship, the Great God commanded a Khasi man and a foreigner to appear before Him on a certain day, upon a certain mountain, the name of which is not known, that they might learn His laws and statutes.

So the Khasi and the foreigner went into the mountain and appeared before God. They remained with Him three days and three nights, and He revealed unto them the mode of worship.

The Great God wrote His laws in books, and at the end of the third day He gave unto each man a book of the holy law, and said unto them: "This is sufficient unto you; return unto your own people; behold, I have written all that is needful for you to know in this book. Take it, and read it, and teach it to your kindred that they may learn how to be wise and holy and happy for ever." The two men took their books and departed as they were commanded.

Between the mountain and their homeland there lay a wide river. On their way thither they had waded through it without any difficulty, for the water was low, but on their return journey they found the river in flood and the water so deep that they had to swim across. They were sorely perplexed how to keep their sacred books safe and dry; being devoid of clothing, the men found it difficult to protect them or to cover them safely. The foreigner had long hair, and he took his book and wrapped it in his long hair, which he twisted firmly on the top of his head; but the hair of the Khasi was short, so he could not follow the example of the foreigner, and, not able to think of a better plan, he took the book between his teeth.

The foreigner swam across safely, with his book undamaged, and he went home to his kindred joyfully and taught them wisdom and the mode of worship.

The Khasi, after swimming part of the way, began to flounder, for the current was strong, and his breathing was impeded by the book in his mouth. His head went under water, and the book was reduced to a worthless pulp. He was in great trouble when he saw that the book was destroyed. He determined to return to the mountain to ask the Great God for a new book, so he swam back across the wide river and climbed again to the mountain; but when he reached the place where he had before met God, he found that He had ascended into heaven, and he had to return empty-handed.

When he reached his own country, he summoned together all his kindred and told them all that had happened. They were very sad when they heard that the book was lost, and bewildered because they had no means of enlightenment. They resolved to call a Durbar of all the Khasis to consider how they could carry on their worship in a becoming way and with some uniformity, so as to secure for themselves the three great blessings of humanity—health, wealth, and families.

Since that day the Khasis have depended for their knowledge of sacred worship on the traditions that have come down from one generation to the other from their ancestors who sat in the great Durbar after the sacred book was lost, while the foreigners learn how to worship from books.

XXXII

THE BLESSING OF THE MENDICANT

Part I

Once there lived a very poor family, consisting of a father, mother, an only son, and his wife. They were poorer than any of their neighbours, and were never free from want; they seldom got a full meal, and sometimes they had to go without food for a whole day, while their clothes but barely covered their bodies. No matter how hard they worked, or where they went to cultivate, their crops never succeeded like the crops of their fellow-cultivators in the same locality. But they were good people, and never grumbled or blamed the gods, neither did they ask alms of any one, but continued to work season after season, contented with their poor fare and their half-empty cooking-pots.

One day an aged mendicant belonging to a foreign tribe wandered into their village, begging for food at every house and for a night's shelter. But nobody pitied him or gave him food. Last of all, he came to the dwelling of the poor family, where, as usual, they had not enough food to satisfy their own need, yet when they saw the aged beggar standing outside in the cold, their hearts were filled with pity. They invited him to enter, and they shared their scanty meal with him. "Come," they said, "we have but little to give you, it is true, but it is not right to leave a fellow-man outside to starve to death." So he lodged with them that night.

It happened that the daughter-in-law was absent that night, so that the stranger saw only the parents and their son.

A KHASI INDUSTRY—FRYING FISH IN THE OPEN AIR.

Next morning, when he was preparing to depart, the mendicant spoke many words of peace and goodwill to the family, and blessed them solemnly, expressing his sympathy with them in their poverty and privation. "You have good hearts," he said, "and have not hesitated to entertain a stranger, and have shared with the poor what you yourselves stood in need of. If you wish, I will show you a way by which you may grow rich and prosperous."

They were very glad to hear this, for their long

struggle with poverty was becoming harder and harder to bear, and they responded eagerly, saying, "Show us the way."

Upon this the mendicant opened a small sack which he carried, and took from it a small live coney, which he handed tenderly to the housewife, saying, "This little animal was given to me years ago by a holy man, who told me that if I killed it and cooked its meat for my food I should grow rich. But by keeping the animal alive for many days I became so fond of it that I could not kill it. Now I am old and weak, the day of my death cannot be far off; at my death perhaps the coney may fall into the hands of unscrupulous persons, so I give it to you who are worthy. Do not keep it alive as I did, otherwise you will not be able to kill it and so will never reap the fruits of the virtue it possesses. When wealth comes to you, beware of its many temptations and continue to live virtuously as at present."

He also warned them not to divulge the secret to any one outside the family, or to let any outsiders taste of the magic meat.

When they were alone, the family began to discuss with wonder the words spoken by the mysterious stranger about the strange animal that had been left in their possession. They determined to act on the advice of their late guest, and to kill the coney on that very day, and that the mother should stay at home from her work in the fields to cook the meat against the return of the men in the evening.

Left to herself, the housewife began to paint glowing pictures of the future, when the family would cease to be in want, and would have no need to labour for their food, but would possess abundance of luxuries, and be the envy of all their neighbours. As she abandoned herself to these idle dreams, the evil spirit of avarice entered her heart unknown to her, and changed her into a hard and pitiless woman, destroying all the generous impulses which had sustained her in all their years of poverty and made her a contented and amiable neighbour.

Some time in the afternoon the daughter-in-law returned home, and, noticing a very savoury smell coming from the cooking-pot, she asked her mother-in-law pleasantly what good luck had befallen them, that she had such a good dinner in preparation. To her surprise, instead of a kind and gentle answer such as she had always received from her mother-in-law, she was answered by a torrent of abuse. and told that she was not to consider herself a member of the family, or to expect a share of the dinner, which a holy man had provided for them.

This unmerited unkindness hurt and vexed the younger woman, but, as it is not right to contradict a mother-in-law, she refrained from making any reply, and sat meekly by the fire, and in silence watched the process of cooking going on. She was very hungry, having come from a long journey, and, knowing that there was no other food in the house except that which her mother-in-law was cooking, she determined to try and obtain a little of it unobserved. When the elder woman left the house for a moment she snatched a handful of meat from the pan and ate it quickly, but her mother-in-law caught her chewing, and charged her with having eaten the meat. As she did not deny it, her mother-in-law began to beat her unmercifully, and turned her out of doors in anger,

The ill-treated woman crawled along the path by which her husband was expected to arrive, and sat on the ground, weeping, to await his coming. When he arrived he marvelled to see his wife crying on the roadside, and asked her the reason for it. She was too upset to answer him for a long time, but when at last she was able to make herself articulate, she told him all that his mother had done to her. He became very wroth, and said, "If my mother thinks more of gaining wealth than of respecting my wife, I will leave my mother's house for ever," and he strode away, taking only a brass *lota* (water vessel) for his journey.

Part II

The husband and wife wandered about in the jungle for many days, living on any wild herbs or roots that they could pick up on their way, but all those days they did not see a village or a sign of a human habitation.

One day they happened to come to a very dry and barren hill, where they could get no water, and they began to suffer from thirst. In this arid place a son was born to them, and the young mother seemed likely to die for want of water. The husband roamed in every direction, but saw no water anywhere, until he climbed to the top of a tall tree in order to survey the country, and to his joy saw in the distance a pool of clear water. He hastened down and fetched his *lota*, and proceeded in the direction of the pool. The jungle was so dense that he was afraid of losing his way, so in order to improvise some sort of landmark, he tore his *dottie* (loin-cloth) into narrow strips which he hung on the bushes as he went.

After a long time he reached the pool, where he quenched his thirst and was refreshed. Then he filled his *lota* to return to his languishing wife, but was tempted to take a plunge in the cool water of the pool, for he was hot and dusty from his toilsome walk. Putting his *lota* on the ground and laying his clothes beside it, he plunged into the water, intending to stay only a few minutes.

Now it happened that a great dragon, called U Yak Jakor, lived in the pool, and he rose to the surface upon seeing the man, dragged him down to the bottom, and devoured him.

The anxious wife, parched with thirst, waited expectantly for the return of her husband, but, seeing no sign of him, she determined to go in search of him. So, folding her babe in a cloth, which she tied on her back, she began to trace the path along which she had seen her husband going, and by the help of the strips of cloth on the bushes, she came at last to the spot where her husband's *lota* and his clothes had been left.

At sight of these she was filled with misgivings, and, failing to see her husband anywhere, she began to call out his name, searching for him in all directions. There were no more strips of cloth, so she knew that he had not gone farther.

When U Yak Jakor heard the woman calling, he came up to the surface of the pool, and seeing she was a woman, and alone, he drew near, intending to force her into the water, for the dragon who was the most powerful of all the dragons inside the pool lost his strength whenever he stood on dry land, and could then do no harm to any one.

In her confusion and fear on account of her husband, the woman did not take much notice of U Yak Jakor when he came, but shouted to him to ask if he had not seen a man passing that way; to which he replied that a man had come, who had been taken to the palace of the king beneath the pool. When she heard this she knew that they had come to the pool of U Yak Jakor, and, looking more closely at the being that had approached her, she saw that he was a dragon. She knew also that U Yak Jakor had no strength on dry land, and she lifted her arm with a threatening gesture, upon which he dived into the pool.

By these tokens the woman understood that her husband had been killed by the dragon. Taking up the *lota* and his clothes, she hurried from the fatal spot and beyond the precincts of the dragon's pool, and, after coming to a safe and distant part of the jungle, she threw herself down on the ground in an abandonment of grief. She cried so loud and so bitterly that her babe awoke and cried in sympathy; to her astonishment she saw that his tears turned into lumps of gold as they fell. She knew this to be a token that the blessing of the mendicant, of which her husband had spoken, had rested upon her boy by virtue of the meat she had eaten.

This knowledge cheered and comforted her greatly, for she felt less defenceless and lonely in the dreary forest. After refreshing herself with water from the *lota*, she set out in search of some human habitation, and after a weary search she came at last to a large village, where the Siem (Chief) of that region lived, who, seeing that she possessed much gold, permitted her to dwell there.

Part III

The boy was named U Babam Doh, because of the meat which his mother had eaten. The two lived very happily in this village, the mother leading an industrious life, for she did not wish to depend for their living on the gold gained at the expense of her son's tears. Neither did she desire it to become known that he possessed the magic power to convert his tears into gold, so she instructed her boy never to weep in public, and on every occasion when he might be driven to cry, she told him to go into some secret place where nobody could witness the golden tears. And so anxious was she not to give him any avoidable cause of grief that she concealed from him the story of her past sufferings and his father's tragic fate, and hid from sight the brass *lota* and the clothes she had found by the dragon's pool.

U Babam Doh grew up a fine and comely boy, in whom his mother's heart delighted; he was strong of body and quick of intellect, so that none of the village lads could compete with him, either at work or at play. Among his companions was the Heir-apparent of the State, a young lad about his own age, who, by reason of the many accomplishments of U Babam Doh, showed him great friendliness and favour, so that the widow's son was frequently invited to the Siem's house, and was privileged to attend many of the great State functions and Durbars. Thus he unconsciously became familiar with State questions, and gleaned much knowledge and wisdom, so that he grew up enlightened and discreet beyond many of his comrades.

One day, during the Duali (Hindu gambling festival), his friend the Heir-apparent teased him to join in the game. He had no desire to indulge in any games of luck, and he was ignorant of the rules of all such games, but he did not like to offend his friend by refusing, so he went with him to the gambling field and joined in the play.

At first the Heir-apparent, who was initiating him into the game, played for very small stakes, but, to their mutual surprise, U Babam Doh the novice won at every turn. The Heir-apparent was annoyed at the continual success of his friend, for he himself had been looked upon as the champion player at previous festivals, so, thinking to daunt the spirit of U Babam Doh, he challenged him to risk higher stakes, which, contrary to his expectation, were accepted, and again U Babam Doh won. They played on until at last the Heir-apparent had staked and lost all his possessions; he grew so reckless that in the end he staked his own right of succession to the throne, and lost.

There was great excitement and commotion when it became known that the Heir-apparent had gambled away his birthright; people left their own games, and from all parts of the field they flocked to where the two young men stood. When the Heir-apparent saw that the people were unanimous in blaming him for so recklessly throwing away what they considered his divine endowment, he tried to retrieve his character by abusing his opponent, taunting him with being ignorant of his father's name, and calling him the unlawful son of U Yak Jakor, saying that it was by the dragon's aid he had won all the bets on that day.

This was a cruel and terrible charge from which U Babam Doh recoiled, but as his mother had never revealed to him her history, he was helpless in face of the taunt, to which he had no answer to give. He stood mute and stunned before the crowd, who, when they saw his dismay, at once concluded that the Heir-apparent's charges were well founded. They dragged U Babam Doh before the Durbar, and accused him of witchcraft before the Siem and his ministers.

U Babam Doh, being naturally courageous and resourceful, soon recovered himself, and having absolute confidence in the justice of his cause, he appealed to the Durbar for time to procure proofs, saying that he would give himself up to die at their hands if he failed to substantiate his claim to honour and respectability, and stating that this charge was fabricated by his opponent, who hoped to recover by perfidy what he had lost in fair game.

The Durbar were perplexed by these conflicting charges, but they were impressed by the temperate and respectful demeanour of the young stranger, in comparison with the flustered and rash conduct of the descendant of their own royal house, so they granted a number of days during which U Babam Doh must procure proofs of his innocence or die.

U Babam Doh left the place of Durbar, burning with shame and humiliation for the stigma that had been cast upon him and upon his mother, and came sadly to his house. When his mother saw his livid face she knew that some great calamity had befallen him, and pressed him to tell her about it, but the only reply he would give to all her questions was, "Give me a mat, oh my mother, give me a mat to lie upon"; whereupon she spread a mat for him on the floor, on which he threw himself down in an abandonment of grief. He wept like one that could never be consoled, and as he wept his tears turned into gold, till the mat on which he lay was covered with lumps of gold, such as could not be counted for their number.

Although the mother saw this inexhaustible wealth at her feet she could feel no pleasure in it, owing to her anxiety for her son, who seemed likely to die of grief. After a time she succeeded in calming him, and gradually she drew forth from him the tale of the attack made upon their honour by the Heir-apparent. She began to upbraid herself bitterly for withholding from him their history, and hastily she went to fetch her husband's clothes and the brass *lota* which she had concealed for so many years, and, bringing them to her son, she told him all that had happened to her and to his father, from the day on which the foreign mendicant visited their hut to the time of their coming to their present abode.

U Babam Doh listened with wonder and pity for the mother who had so bravely borne so many sorrows, concealing all her woes in order to spare him all unnecessary pangs. When the mother finished her tale U Babam Doh stood up and shook himself, and, taking his bow and his quiver, he said, "I must go and kill U Yak Jakor, and so avenge my father's death, and vindicate my mother's honour."

The mother's heart was heavy when she saw him depart, but she knew that the day had arrived for him to fulfil his duty to his father's memory, so she made no attempt to detain him, but gave him minute directions about the locality, and the path leading to the dragon's haunts.

Part IV

After a long journey U Babam Doh arrived at the pool, on the shores of which he found a large wooden chest, which he rightly guessed had belonged to some unfortunate traveller who had fallen a victim to the dragon. Upon opening the chest he found it full of fine clothes and precious stones, such as are worn only by great princes; these he took and made into a bundle to bring home.

Remembering his mother's instructions not to venture into the pool, he did not leave the dry land, although he was hot and tired and longed to bathe in order to refresh himself. He began to call out with a loud voice as if hallooing to some lost companions, and this immediately attracted to the surface U Yak Jakor, who, after waiting a while to see if the man would not come to bathe in the pool, came ashore, thinking to lure his prey into the water. But U Babam Doh was on his guard, and did not stir from his place, and when the dragon came within reach he attacked him suddenly and captured him alive. He then bound him with rattan and confined him in the wooden chest.

Fortified by his success, and rejoicing in his victory, U Babam Doh took the chest on his shoulders and brought the dragon home alive. Being wishful to enhance the sensation, when the day came for him to make his revelations public in the Durbar, he did not inform his mother that he had U Yak Jakor confined in the wooden chest, and when she questioned him about the contents of the chest he was silent, promising to let her see it some day. In the meantime he forbade her to open it, on pain of offending him, but he showed her the bundle of silken clothes.

The news soon spread through the village that U Babam Doh had come back, and when the people saw him walking with lifted head and steadfast look, the rumour got abroad that he had been successful in his quest for proofs. This rumour caused the Heir-apparent to tremble for his own safety, and hoping to baulk U Babam Doh once more, he persuaded the Siem to postpone the date of the Durbar time after time. Thus U Yak Jakor remained for many days undiscovered, confined in the chest.

Now U Babam Doh's mother, being a woman, was burning with curiosity to know the secret of that wooden chest which her son had brought home and around which there appeared so much mystery. One day, when her son was absent, she determined to peep into it to see what was hidden there. U Yak Jakor had overheard all that the mother and son had said to one another, and he knew that the woman was not aware of his identity. As soon as he heard her approaching the chest he quickly transformed himself into the likeness of her dead husband, though he was powerless to break the rattan.

The woman was startled beyond speech when she saw (as she thought) her husband alive and almost unchanged, whom she had mourned as dead for so many long years. When she could control her joy she requested him to come out, to partake of food and betel nut, but he replied that although he had by the help of their son escaped from the dragon's stronghold, he was under certain vows which would have to be fulfilled before he could come out, for if he left the chest before the fulfilment of his vow he would fall again into the power of the dragon.

The mother began to find fault with her son for having concealed the fact of her husband's rescue from her, but the dragon said that if the son had disclosed the fact to anybody before the fulfilment of the vows it would have committed him into U Yak Jakor's hands. She must beware of letting U Babam Doh know that she had discovered the secret, or both her son and her husband would be lost to her for ever, while by judicious help she might bring about his release.

Upon hearing this the woman implored him to show her in what way she could assist, and so quicken his release. The wily dragon hoped in this way to bring about the death of U Babam Doh, so he replied that his vow involved drinking a seer of tigress' milk, and that he who obtained the milk must not know for whom or for what purpose it was obtained.

This was sad news for the woman, for it seemed to her quite impossible to procure tigress' milk on any condition. She was even less likely to find any one willing to risk his life to get it, without knowing for whom and for what purpose, and she wept bitterly. After a time she called to mind the many exploits of her son as a hunter, and she conceived a sudden plan by which she hoped to obtain tigress' milk.

By and by she heard the footsteps of her son outside, and she hurriedly closed the lid of the chest, and lay on the ground, and feigned sickness, writhing as if in great agony. U Babam Doh was much concerned when he saw his mother, and bent over her with great solicitude. He tried many remedies, but she seemed to grow worse and worse, and he cried out in sorrow, saying, "Tell me, my mother, what remedy will cure you, and I will get it or die."

"It is written in my *nusip* (book of fate) that I shall die of this sickness, unless I drink a seer of tigress' milk," said the mother.

"I will obtain for you some tigress' milk," said the youth, "or die"; and, taking his bow and quiver and his father's *lota*, he went into the forest, asking some neighbours to come and sit with his mother during his absence.

When he had been gone some time his mother said she felt better, and requested the neighbours to return to their homes, as she wished to sleep; but as soon as they were out of earshot she got up and prepared a savoury meal for him whom she thought her husband.

Part V

U Babam Doh, eager to see his mother healed, walked without halting till he came to a dense and uninhabited part of the forest which he thought might be the haunt of wild beasts, but he could see no trail of tigers. He was about to return home after a fruitless hunt, as he feared to be absent too long from his mother, when he heard loud moans from behind a near thicket. He immediately directed his steps towards the sound, prepared to render what assistance he could to whoever was suffering. To his surprise he found some young tiger cubs, one of whom had swallowed a bone, which had stuck in his throat, and was choking him. U Babam Doh quickly made a pair of pincers from a piece of bamboo, and soon had the bone removed. The cubs were very thankful for the recovery of their brother, and showed their gratitude by purring and licking U Babam Doh's hand, while the cub from whose throat the bone was extracted crouched at his feet, declaring that he would be his attendant for ever.

U Babam Doh took up his *lota* and his bow and prepared to depart, but the cubs entreated him to stay until their mother returned, so as to get her permission for the young tiger to follow him. So U Babam Doh stayed with the cubs to await the return of the tigress.

Before long the muffled sound of her tread was heard approaching. As she drew near, she sniffed the air suspiciously, and soon detected the presence of a man in her lair. Putting herself in a fighting attitude, she began to growl loudly, saying, "Human flesh, human flesh"; but the cubs ran to meet her, and told her how a kind man had saved their brother from death. Whereupon she stopped her growling, and, like her cubs, she showed her gratitude to U Babam Doh by purring and licking his hands.

The tigress asked him many questions, for it was a rare occurrence for a man to wander so far into the jungle alone. On being told that he had come in search of tigress' milk to save his mother's life, she exclaimed eagerly that she knew of a way to give him what he wanted, by which she could in some measure repay him for saving her cub, and she bade him bring his *lota* and fill it with milk from her dugs. U Babam Doh did as she told him, and obtained abundance of tigress' milk, with which he hastened home to his mother, accompanied by the tiger cub.

Part VI

U Babam Doh found his mother, on his return, in just the same condition as when he left her; so as soon as he arrived he put the *lota* of milk into her hand, and said, "Drink, oh my mother. I have obtained for you some tigress' milk, drink and live." She made a pretence of drinking, but as soon as her son left the house she hurried to the wooden chest, and, handing in the *lota*, she said, "Drink, oh my husband. Our son hath obtained the tigress' milk, drink and be free from the dragon's power."

U Yak Jakor was vexed to find that U Babam Doh had returned unharmed, and began to think how he could send him on another perilous venture, and he answered the woman plaintively, "To drink tigress' milk is only a part of my vow; before I can be released from the dragon's power I must anoint my body with fresh bear's grease, and he who obtains it for me must not know for whom or for what purpose it is obtained."

The woman was very troubled to hear this, for she feared to send her son into yet another danger, but, believing that there was no other way to secure her husband's release, she again feigned sickness, and when her son asked her why the tigress' milk had not effected a cure, she replied:

"It is written in my *nusip* that I must die of this sickness unless I anoint my body with fresh bear's grease."

"I will obtain the fresh bear's grease for you, oh my mother, or die," answered the youth impetuously; and once more he started to the forest, taking his bow and quiver, and his father's *lota*, which he had filled with honey.

As he was starting off, the tiger cub began to follow him, but U Babam Doh commanded him to stop at home to guard the house, and went alone to the forest. After travelling far he saw the footprints of bears, whereupon he cut some green plaintain leaves and spread them on the ground and poured the honey upon them, and went to hide in the thicket. Soon a big bear came and began to eat the honey greedily, and while it was busy feasting, U Babam Doh, from behind the thicket, threw a thong round its throat and captured it alive. Upon this a fierce struggle began; but the bear, finding that the more he struggled the tighter the grip on his throat became, was soon subdued, and was led a safe, though unwilling captive by U Babam Doh out of the jungle. Thus once again the son brought to his mother the remedy which was supposed to be written in her *nusip*.

When he came in sight of his home, leading the bear by the thong, the tiger cub, on seeing his master, ran to meet him, with the good news that his mother had recovered and had been cooking savoury meals for a guest who was staying in the house. This news cheered U Babam Doh greatly, and, fastening the bear to a tree, he hastened to the house to greet his mother, but to his disappointment he found her ill and seemingly in as much pain as ever. Without delay he took a knife and went out to kill the bear, and, filling the *lota* with grease, he brought it to his mother, saying:

"Anoint yourself, oh my mother, I have obtained for you the bear's grease; anoint yourself and live."

He then went out to seek the tiger cub and punish him for deceiving him about his mother's condition, but the cub declared on oath that he had spoken only the truth, and that his mother had really been entertaining a guest during her son's absence, and seemed to have been in good health, going about her work, and cooking savoury meals.

U Babam Doh was greatly mystified; he was loth to believe his mother could be capable of any duplicity, and yet the tiger cub seemed to speak the truth. He determined not to say anything to his mother about the matter, but to keep a watch on her movements for a few days.

When her son left the house after giving her the bear's grease, the woman rose quickly, and lifting the lid of the chest, she said:

"Anoint yourself, oh my husband. Our son hath obtained the bear's grease; anoint yourself and be free from the dragon's power."

As before, the dragon was again very chagrined to find that U Babam Doh had come back alive and uninjured, so he thought of yet another plan by which he could send him into a still greater danger, and he answered the woman: "Anointing my body with bear's grease is only a part of my vow; before I can be released from the dragon's power I must be covered for one whole night with the undried skin of a python, and he who obtains the skin for me must not know for what purpose or for whom it is obtained."

The woman wept bitterly when she heard of this vow, for she feared to send her son among the reptiles. U Yak Jakor, seeing her hesitation, began to coax her, and to persuade her to feign sickness once again, and she, longing to see her husband released, yielded to his coaxing. When her son came in he found her seemingly worse than he had seen her before, and once more he knelt by her side and begged of her to tell him what he could do for her that would ease her pain.

She replied, "It is written in my *nusip* that I must die of this sickness unless I am covered for a whole night with the undried skin of a python"; and as before U Babam Doh answered and said that he would obtain for her whatever was written in her *nusip*; but he did not say that he would bring a python skin.

Taking his bow and quiver, he left the house, as on former occasions, and walked in the direction of the jungle, but this time he did not proceed far. He returned home unobserved, and, climbing to the roof of the house, he quietly removed some of the thatch, which enabled him to see all that was going on inside the house, while he himself was unseen.

Very soon he saw his mother getting up, as if in her usual health, and preparing to cook a savoury meal, which, to his amazement, when it had been cooked, she took to the wooden chest where he knew the dragon to be confined. As he looked, he saw the figure of a man lying in the chest, and he knew then that U Yak Jakor had transformed himself into another likeness in order to dupe his mother. He listened, and soon he understood from their conversation that the dragon had taken the form of his own dead father, and by that means had succeeded in making his mother a tool against her own son. He now blamed himself for not having confided to his mother the secret of the chest, and determined to undeceive her without further delay.

He entered the house quickly, before his mother had time to close the lid of the chest. She stood before him flustered and confused, thinking that by her indiscretion she had irrevocably committed her husband to the power of the dragon; but when U Babam Doh informed her of the deception played upon her by U Yak Jakor she was overwhelmed with terror, to think how she had been duped into sending her brave son into such grave perils, and abetting the dragon in his evil designs on his life.

When U Yak Jakor saw that there was no further advantage to be gained by keeping the man's form he assumed his own shape, and, thinking to prevent them from approaching near enough to harm him, he emitted the most foul stench from his scaly body. But U Babam Doh, who had borne so much, was not to be thwarted, and without any more lingering he took the chest on his shoulders and carried it to the place of Durbar. There, before the Siem and his ministers and the whole populace, he recounted the strange story of his own adventures and his parents' history. At the end of the tale he opened the wooden chest and exhibited the great monster, who had been such a terror to travellers for many generations, and in the presence of the Durbar, amid loud cheers, he slew U Yak Jakor, and so avenged his father's death and vindicated his mother's honour.

The Siem and the Durbar unanimously appointed him the Heir-apparent, and when in the course of time he succeeded to the throne he proved himself a wise and much-loved ruler, who befriended the poor and the down-trodden and gave shelter to the stranger and the homeless. He always maintained that his own high estate was bestowed upon him in consequence of his family's generosity to a lonely and unknown mendicant, whose blessing descended upon them and raised them from a state of want and poverty to the highest position in the land.